THE SCIENCE OF
ON-CAMERA ACTING

THE SCIENCE OF ON-CAMERA ACTING

ANDRÉA MORRIS

WITH COMMENTARY BY DR. PAUL EKMAN

Published by Becoming Media

ISBN 978-0-9907332-1-8

Library of Congress Control Number: 2014914093
LCCN Imprint Name: Becoming Media Production and Publishing Company,
Los Angeles, CA

Typesetting services by BOOKOW.COM

ACKNOWLEDGMENTS

Special thanks to my wonderful family, especially my beloved parents and gifted husband. Thanks to my C.S. editor Joe, and to Steve Passiouras at bookow.com for his keen eye, artful touch, and for going above and beyond. Thanks also to the many fine actors I've had the honor of experimenting with over the years. Lastly, much thanks to Dr. Paul Ekman for his insights into the art of screen acting and his contributions to this book.

NOTE TO THE READER

Printed editions of this book use a contemporary model, Print on Demand (POD). This allows for more affordable book prices and helps the environment by saving trees. Although errors in printing are rare, POD does experience them at a slightly higher rate than with larger print runs. If this occurs, please contact Becoming Media Production and Publishing to receive a free replacement copy.

www.BecomingMedia.com

Contents

PART I

WHAT THE CAMERA SEES

The *I* of the Camera

"WHAT is it that drew you to study the human face?" I ask Dr. Paul Ekman, the pioneer of micro expressions who inspired the Fox TV series *Lie to Me* starring Tim Roth. Named by the American Psychological Association as one of the top one hundred most influential psychologists of the twentieth century, Dr. Ekman consults with police officers, FBI and CIA agents, and politicians. His research revolutionized our understanding of the science of facial expression and emotion. Most recently his work with the Dalai Lama was published in the 2008 book *Emotional Awareness*. With an enthusiasm that catalyzed a decryption system for the human face, he answers my question. "I just can't think of anything that's more fascinating. I mean, when you think of what the face does, it's our primary signal-system for identity. It's how we tell one person from another. We don't do it by smell as other animals do. We do it by the appearance of their face, all the variation in their features and the location and shape that gives everybody a different look. That's sort of a stage, and on this stage you have these expressions temporarily changing the appearance of these features. And then you have the primary sensory organs, sight, and hearing, speaking. So the face is an amazingly complicated and commanding system. We know from neuroscience research that there's a very large part of the brain dedicated to dealing with the face because of this richness of information." He pauses. "So I can't understand why everyone isn't studying the face."

* * *

Applying the scientific method to art lets us distinguish between creative processes that generate results, and those that are redundant, misguided, or worse yet, inhibit the artist and must be unlearned. The following principles applied to screen acting focus exclusively on what works for the camera and provide insight into the technological mediator between you and your audience, giving actor and director an understanding of what's taking place in translation. Yet the uniqueness of each performance underscores the crucial fact that the scientific model doesn't sterilize art. Instead, science dissolves the scaffolding of dogma and grants unobstructed access to a moment infused with impulse and creativity, where something seemingly irreducible and ineffable emerges.

When applied to the arts, science offers conduits to inspiration completely outside its own analytic structure. Some may see science and the arts as a counterintuitive coupling. They are, in fact, worthy collaborators.

The Science of On-Camera Acting is predicated on pragmatism and simplification. With that in mind, it must be said that an actor's method is ultimately whatever works best for the actor. I personally define "whatever works" as whatever produces great on-camera performances and doesn't make you miserable.

I encourage you to experiment on-camera, testing this approach against others. I'm fascinated by how and why things work, but learning something *that* works is the chief concern of this book. The development of this method didn't begin with an ounce of theory; it was all on-camera work, experimentation using visual, camera-based biofeedback. There was no time to invent actor problems. As you will see, almost every classic acting problem can be overcome in twenty minutes or less. This book isn't about quick fixes for big problems, but if there's a quick fix for a problem, maybe it was never as big as it seemed.

"The invention of the camera has changed not only what we see, but how we see it."

John Berger, author and BAFTA Award winner for his BBC series *Ways of Seeing*, speaking about the actor's most important collaborator[1]

The T on the ground was bright-neon blue, taped to the linoleum only moments before, but was already curling up along the edges where I'd kneaded it with the tip of a pristine white sneaker. I was twelve, on the set of my first film. I watched as everyone involved in the production functioned like cells in a body, working together to bring about a rich sensory experience. In the center of the dither was a quiet, mysterious, mechanical eye, like the eye at the center of a tornado, its perspective driving everything whirling around it. I stared at this mountain of machinery with its silvery lens reflecting rings that disappeared into blackness.

The camera's eye seemed inscrutable. When sneaking in to watch dailies, what I saw on the screen differed from my memory of what we had shot just hours earlier.[2] The difference between the actor's perspective and the camera's perspective of the exact same event raised

---

[1] Berger, John. Ways of Seeing: Based on the BBC Television Series with John Berger. (London: British Broadcasting Corporation, 1990).

[2] We're becoming a little more familiar with the dissociative phenomena via daily photos and videos of ourselves on social media.

questions that seemed important for someone wanting to do this professionally.

One afternoon, I was strapped in a corset and other apparel from the nineteenth century, sitting in the dining nook of a trailer and listening to a science show on CBC radio. The guest was talking about how phenomena in our natural world that seem chaotic and haphazard are actually orderly; all it takes is a shift in our perspective. I wondered if the camera's perspective had more to teach us than what most of us were paying attention to.

Many filmmakers have found the camera's eye beguiling. In his 1923 manifesto *Kino Eye* (translation *Cinema Eye*), Russian director Dziga Vertov wrote:

"I am an eye. A mechanical eye. I, the machine, show
you a world the way only I can see it. I free myself for
today and forever from human immobility. I'm in
constant movement. I approach and pull away from
objects. I creep under them. I move alongside a
running horse's mouth. I fall and rise with the falling
and rising bodies. This is I, the machine, maneuvering
in the chaotic movements, recording one movement
after another in the most complex combinations.
Freed from the boundaries of time and space. I co
-ordinate any and all points of the universe, wherever I
want them to be. My way leads towards the creation of
a fresh perception of the world. Thus, I explain in a
new way the world unknown to you."[3]

---

[3] Vertov, Dziga, and Annette Michelson. Kino-eye: The Writings of Dziga Vertov. (Berkeley, CA: University of California Press, 1984).

Early on I was fortunate to work with acclaimed actors who shared numerous tips and insights, and I watched them integrate their creative impulses into the framework of a highly technical medium. The opportunity to engage with pros was invaluable, and similar expert advice is widely available on *Inside the Actors Studio* and various other interview shows, blogs, podcasts and news outlets. Yet, for the amount of time actors spend working to surmount the odds, there is sparse discussion about how to prevail over the monolithic barrier to entry into a field saturated with competition: The audition process demands that you juggle every kind of role in every type of project being thrown at you with only a day to prepare. It requires that you cultivate a tremendous amount of grit under pressure while staying open and vulnerable. And it demands you do all this exceedingly well on-camera. The standby cold reading and audition workshops are eager to address these challenges, and most offer theories with helpful highlights. Yet they ultimately come up short when applied to the daily variables of working and auditioning.

"All children are artists. The problem is how to remain
an artist once he grows up…It took me four years to
paint like Raphael, but a lifetime to paint like a child."

Pablo Picasso[4]

As a child I quickly learned that for most roles the choices were simple and fairly obvious. Be yourself. React honestly, in the moment, truthfully. No problem. I got that. I was a kid. That sort of thing comes easily for kids. But once in a while I'd get auditions for roles I couldn't make work. These were instances where playing the "truth"

---

[4] Picasso, Pablo, "The Artist Pablo Picasso" www.theartistpablopicasso.com/pablo-picasso-painting -Les-Demoiselles-dAvignon.htm, accessed July 6, 2014.

of the moment didn't seem to be enough. My agent said this reflected a lack of experience and the difference between an actor with natural instincts and a trained actor. I signed up for acting classes, attended a school for the arts, and lived in New York City in the summer while attending the American Academy of the Dramatic Arts youth program.

In exact parallel to my creative education, any natural ability I'd started with quickly devolved into something muddled and stilted. The training created an out-of-body experience from the character, detached from its core, floating above it on the operating table, dissecting it with my mind while it lay there, lifeless. The paradox of working to improve skills and getting to use those skills professionally, while unwittingly neutering any creativity, brought on a certain level of anxiety that culminated in a wooden performance featured at a Toronto Film Festival Gala Premiere. It was an eminently unflattering teenage nightmare being played out on a fifty-foot screen for 2,630 audience members.

"I learned much more about acting from philosophy courses, psychology courses, history, and anthropology than I ever learned in acting class."

Tim Robbins[5]

Things went from bad to worse, but I was too stubborn to let humiliation stop me. In my midteens I relocated to Los Angeles where I'd only get callbacks for characters who were completely traumatized. I took a break from acting and enrolled in college, where my underused cognitive skills stretched their figurative legs and ran off some steam.

[5] Robbins, Tim, "Tim Robbins Director - Interviews." Industry Central, www.industrycentral.net/director_interviews/TR01.HTM, accessed August 6, 2014.

Over the next four years I focused on philosophy and science, recovering from my acting training by forgetting it. Dr. Ekman's work was featured prominently in psychology courses and offered a deeper understanding of the intricacies taking place watching a face in close-up.

Philosophy of mind explored theories about who we are, and physiological psychology offered scientific studies that tested important parts of these theories. Then one day I was struck by a communication breakdown between departments. We were arguing the logical validity of a clever theory of mind in philosophy class, while neuroscience had abandoned it because it had been proven to have nothing to do with how the brain actually works. This departure from common sense—theory not keeping up with scientific progress—and the gap between the sciences and humanities[6] made me wonder what impact this had on acting training.

"I became a scientist in my process..."

Matthew McConaughey[7]

---

[6] Kostarelos, Kostas, "I Have a Dream, that One Day Scientists and Philosophers will Join Hands," theguardian.com, www.theguardian.com/science/small-world/2013/dec/19/scientists-philosophers-sciences-humanities-nanotechnology, accessed July 6, 2014.

[7] Whipp, Glenn, "Matthew McConaughey's Advice for a Career McConaissance," www.latimes.com/entertainment/envelope/moviesnow/la-et-mn-matthew-mcconaughey-20131114,0,5190927.story#ixzz2rBzk1WhC, accessed July 6, 2014.

Problems with Traditional Analytic Approaches

IF traditional training has served you swimmingly, then wonderful. As we established, the most important thing is whatever works for you. But if you find yourself relating to some of the struggles traditional approaches can concuss, it's unlikely a failing on your part as much as contemporary training being out of touch with what science now tells us about ourselves. The birth of modern neuroscience happened around the same time the major acting approaches were popularized. What we now know about the brain is light years from what we knew when the field was first established. Yet the vast majority of acting training today is some derivation of older acting approaches that were based on misguided psychological tropes of their time.

A reliance on language and concepts

I am of the school of thought that the actor's job is to serve the story and language of the script. Paradoxically however, the actor's work is nonlinguistic. This distinction is often overlooked to the detriment of an actor in training. The standard model for teaching and learning relies on language and concepts, while evidence increasingly suggests an actor's most powerful creative resources are located in a part of the brain that can't process language or concepts. One of the biggest problems with the standard teaching paradigm's reliance on language and concepts is that:

"When pressure-filled situations create an inner monologue of worries in your head that taps verbal brainpower, performing activities that also rely heavily on these same verbal resources is more difficult."

Sian Beilock, cognitive scientist[8]

In other words, breaking down a scene's subtext, objectives, obstacles, and backstory, and memorizing lines, etc., all use concepts and language that draw from the verbal part of your brain. Yet your inner critic is also verbal, and draws from this same region of the brain, using up finite brainpower. When worries enter your brain and your inner critic starts chattering, there's finite verbal brainpower left over, and verbal worry will push out the verbal work. Think of your inner critic as a rhinoceros and the analytic-acting homework as an aardvark. Both are competing to drink from a tiny watering hole in the sweltering Savanna. Who is going to get the water? Who is going to get squashed trying?

Creativity and working memory

It's a common figure of speech, but ultimately it is misleading to talk about the right side of your brain as creative and the left as analytic. A summary of studies compiled by Scott Barry Kaufman in his review in *Scientific American*[9] talks about multiple neural networks at play when creative juices are flowing. However, traditional training for actors tends to place emphasis on a central intellectual faculty of mind: **working memory**. Working memory is the root of our conscious awareness, our identity, the "I" in "I think therefore I am."

---

[8] Beilock, Sian, Choke (Carlton, Victoria: Melbourne University Press, 2011), 130.
[9] Barry Kaufman, Scott, "The Real Neuroscience of Creativity: Beautiful Minds, Scientific American Blog Network," Scientific American Global RSS. blogs.scientificamerican.com/beautiful -minds/2013/08/19/the-real-neuroscience-of-creativity/, accessed July 6, 2014.

"Working memory is that part of your consciousness
that you're aware of at any given time…It's not
something you can turn off. If you turn it off that's
called a coma."

Dr. Peter Doolittle, Virginia Tech Professor of
Education Psychology[10]

Working memory is how we focus on the task at hand, and also how we keep more than one thing in our mind at one time. Working memory holds high esteem in our culture. When your IQ is tested, it is your working memory that is being tested. Working memory is where things pass through your awareness, but it's not where anything stays. Eventually new skills are delegated to more powerful areas of the brain, where feats both simple and great can be executed unconsciously. In other words, skills are delivered *from* your conscious and explicit working memory *to* your unconscious, implicit memory, where the journal *Frontiers in Behavioral Neuroscience* says, "perceptual priming, contextual priming and classical conditioning for emotional stimuli" take place.[11] Working memory is pretty remarkable, but our individual capacity for working memory varies between weak and extremely weak. It used to be believed that working memory allows most of us to hold up to seven things in our head at one time, but neuroimaging now suggests it's more like four.[12] Think of the majesty and weakness

---

[10] Doolittle, Peter, "How your 'Working Memory' Makes Sense of the World," www.ted.com/talks/peter_doolittle_how_your_working_memory_makes_sense_of_the_world.html, accessed July 6, 2014.

[11] Luethi, Mathias, Beat Meier, and Carmen Sandi, "Stress Effects on Working Memory, Explicit Memory, and Implicit Memory For Neutral and Emotional Stimuli in Healthy Men," Frontiers in Behavioral Neuroscience, 2.

[12] Doolittle, Peter, "How Your 'Working Memory' Makes Sense of the World," www.ted.com/talks/peter_doolittle_how_your_working_memory_makes_sense_of_the_world.html, accessed July 6, 2014.

of working memory like the majesty and fragility of a hummingbird. Hummingbirds are almost chimerical creatures, able to hover in the air with their tiny wings batting seventy times per second, but they're also quite fragile.

When you first learn a new task, like driving, you use working memory to consciously execute every step. Because working memory is limited, you make a lot of mistakes when you're learning. Working memory is inextricably linked with your inner critic, who is well aware of these mistakes and the limitations of working memory. This is why you're self-conscious of your every move, resulting in jerky, curb-clipping, "nervous driving." As you become more skilled, unconscious, implicit procedural memory takes over for working memory, smoothing out the bumps. If you are an experienced driver, procedural memory allows you to drive across town, maneuvering through innumerable life-threatening hazards, daydreaming through your entire commute and arriving at your destination with almost no memory of the trip. When skills are ingrained and removed from working memory, we tend to experience them as naturally and reflexively as instincts.

Although working memory is critical for learning, in a creative context it functions optimally when in balance with other mental faculties. However, the vast majority of acting training tends to throw off this balance by placing emphasis on the intellect, on using working memory to analyze, conceptualize, and verbalize reflexes, emotions, impulses, and instincts, making them abstract and putting actors in their heads. It's imperative to note that all analytic-acting approaches —approaches that use language and concepts for analyzing and creating backstories, inner monologues, and subtext, and for defining obstacles, wants, needs, objectives, etc.—rely heavily on working memory.

"Psychological scientists find that while increased working memory capacity seems to boost mathematical problem solving, it might actually get in the way of creative problem solving."

Association for Psychological Science[13]

Analytic approach's reliance on working memory

An overemphasis on working memory has come at a price for actors. Common acting exercises conceptualize human experiences by taking natural, spontaneous, reflexive experiences—such as listening, reacting, feeling, and expressing emotion—and serving them up for contemplation. The very act of isolating instinctual aspects of ourselves and examining them under a microscope alters their nature, because it brings them back into awkward working memory.

You've probably been in a class practicing listening exercises and been the recipient of stellar listening executed by a grade-A acting student. The class likely had the importance of listening explained to them, and this student is now explicitly working at listening, with their head slightly cocked, penetrating you with their eyes—the very same markers used in clinical psychology to identify psychopaths. "The particular stare of the psychopath…is an intense, relentless gaze…as if the psychopath is directing all of his intensity toward you through his eyes."[14] Scientist Robert Hare, author of the official Psychopathy Checklist, refers to the psychopath's stare as, "Intense eye contact and piercing eyes."[15]

---

[13] Association for Psychological Science, "Greater Working Memory Capacity Benefits Analytic, but Not Creative, Problem-Solving," ScienceDaily, www.sciencedaily.com/releases/2012/08/120807132209.htm, accessed July 6, 2014.

[14] Jones, Mizzie, Mask of Sanity, February 19, 2009, masksofsanity.blogspot.com/2009/02/stare-of -psychopath-whats-beneath-it.html, accessed March 7, 2014.

[15] Hare, Robert as quoted by Mizzie Jones, "Mask of Sanity," February 19, 2009, masksofsanity.blogspot.com/2009/02/stare-of-psychopath-whats-beneath-it.html, accessed March 7, 2014.

Psychopaths often have to feign certain emotions and corresponding expressions because they are incapable of actually feeling and reacting to them. Their lack of empathy limits their capacity to connect emotionally to others. Therefore, many of their behaviors that should be unconscious and reflexive are *acts*. They use their working memory to consciously execute the task of listening, resulting in the overly affected gaze. Psychopaths can be incredibly charismatic, but they also frequently induce degrees of discomfort in others. This is because the majority of people are fairly good at sensing when natural human responses are contrived.

The focus on listening is propagated by the acting aphorism that *acting is about listening*. In an interview, Ethan Hawke offers insights he gleaned from shooting the dialogue-intensive, Academy-Award-nominated *Before Sunrise* film trilogy with director Richard Linklater:

"Actors always talk about listening and stuff, but Rick's always reminding us that, 'you know what, you're not actually listening. From this moment forward you're planning what you're going to say and you're waiting for a pause long enough to get it in.'"[16]

An interesting experiment is to use a smartphone to film yourself and other consenting friends in a context where you can forget the camera is on. During playback, watch what happens when you are actually listening.

Emotion

If the body is the actor's tool, this tool differs from all others in its ability to feel and express emotion. Yet there are few groups of people with

---

[16] Mitchell, Elvis, KCRW The Treatment with Elvis Mitchell, June 3, 2013.

more emotional blocks than actors. Actors are constantly working to evoke, manipulate, master, and even fake emotion. This emphasis is in direct opposition to the very nature of emotion. Emotional blocks arise because actors spend so much energy putting their emotions under the spotlight of working memory.

Impulse

Impulses are unconscious reactions and urges. They signify our true feelings, fears, and desires. Our impulses broadcast who we really are and are filtered through our inner critic, so that we may survive in a socially advanced society. Our true selves are usually only embraced in specific contexts. One of these contexts is acting for the screen. When we talk about an actor and "truth" we are talking about actors expressing these uncensored impulses. Filtering impulse filters honesty. When watching an actor perform we crave an honest, unfiltered display of impulse and emotion.

The value of some analytic-acting exercises can be found in their ability to distract your inner critic while impulse tiptoes by, trying not to disturb it. Yet you may have found that when the stakes are high, your inner critic rears its ugly head and freezes impulse in its tracks. This is even the case when a particular analytic technique requires that the actor "forget the work." Forgetting the work can be interpreted as yet another task for your already-overwhelmed working memory. It's the **try not to think of a pink elephant** or **ironic process theory** that describes the **ironic rebound** of unwanted thoughts. "Ironic processing is the psychological process whereby an individual's deliberate attempts to suppress or avoid certain thoughts (thought suppression) render those thoughts more persistent."[17] Telling you to forget the work is like telling you not to look down if you're walking a tightrope. An even safer bet is to get your feet on firm ground.

---

[17] Wikipedia contributors, Ironic Process Theory, Wikipedia, the Free Encyclopedia, en.wikipedia.org/wiki/Ironic_process_theory, accessed July 6, 2014.

Trying versus struggling

The word *try* has two different meanings in a creative context. Trying something new for the purpose of experimentation and exploration is the constructive kind of trying. This kind of trying is the basis for discovery and how actors grow. It is the kind of trying done while the pressure is off, when there isn't immediate pressure to produce results. Trying to coax something that you fear won't come without exerting effort is the other kind of trying. The latter is trying for specific effect. The pressure of trying to achieve a specific result creates anxiety that poses a unique hazard for screen actors. When pressure is on, our faces often engage in something called **involuntary leakage.** This is a "leaked" facial expression revealing the pressure you are feeling and whatever other emotions you are trying to conceal or work through as you seek to center yourself in the character and the scene. When you exert effort in almost any other profession, leakage is not a problem. In screen acting, what's happening on your face *is* your work, so involuntary leakage is problematic. Trying for effect can also occur when an actor tries to stir something in another actor or in their audience. This kind of trying pierces the veil of the character, revealing the actor's insecurities beneath. It advertises the actor's struggle for results.

Another problem with trying for effect is that it assumes that what's going on in the moment isn't good enough. It may not be, but the effort that ensues is not the answer. As soon as you feel the urge to work, trying sets up the opponent on the other end of a game of tug -of-war. One end is where you are, and the other is where you think you should be. This opposition clogs impulse. An example of the unhelpful kind of trying is seen in countless exercises designed to ground you in the emotional "reality" of the scene. These exercises require that you focus on some external memory or endow your acting partner with traits from some imagined or remembered person. I don't think it's the best use of creative energy to leave the moment to conjure some memory from your past. Nor abandon the moment by throwing imagined emotional wallpaper over everything. If you are trying to bedazzle or block out what is going on around you, you are creating that tug-of -war by fighting for a made-up scenario over reality, when your job is to turn make-believe *into* reality. This may seem like only a semantic distinction, but it has real ramifications. Trying to cover the moment with memories or fantasies is often stressful to the actor and painful to watch. Staying out of your head means no longer trying to deny any part of the moment with a memory or fantasy. With the method in this book, you will be trying for discovery, not trying for results. By trying for discovery, the desired results follow expeditiously.

Make your audience lean in

Many actors, particularly in auditions, have a tendency to lean forward, jutting their chin out when speaking their lines. This is often predicated on a direction that an actor must *do* something to the other character and *do* something to their audience. Actors are often told they must try to convince, try to get what they want, try to listen, or try to communicate their need. All this effort causes actors to lean forward. There's nothing mysterious about effort. It broadcasts your need to please. When you stop trying, you stop showing, and you become interesting. As a result, you stop leaning forward and those watching your work lean in.

The value of nonanalytic creativity

In many ways acting shares qualities and challenges similar to meditation. Monks of Eastern religions and philosophies refer to the train of thought constantly racing through our heads as the thinker or monkey mind. As we try to meditate, the thinker generally struggles for something to do and gets in our way. Likewise, the thinker often interrupts an actor's creative flow. Meditation, like acting, follows the same simple-isn't-easy principle. Mastery involves a great deal of practice and honoring a part of the mind separate from the thinker. This part of the mind is frequently undervalued in modern Western cultures, where the classic analytic definition of intelligence still reigns supreme. Nonanalytic creative contributions are often discredited even among artists. Emphasis on working memory is the chorus of our inner critic, adept at heralding analytic contributions and trouncing impulse. Actors sometimes feel insecure if they are not contributing in a way that involves the intellect. There is a fear that this perhaps reduces actors to puppets of the writer and director. But the confusion undermines the significant contribution within the actor's domain. Embracing unconscious, moment-to-moment creative impulse under utterly fabricated circumstances is the actor's most challenging endeavor, not to be cheapened or unsung. The actor's duties are unique and differ from many of those handled by the writer and the director's explicit working memory. What actors do is more closely related to abstract painting than writing. Actors, as well as their collaborators, need to halt the trend of undermining creative contributions that lie principally outside the scope of language, concepts, and analytic working memory.

"Athletes under pressure sometimes try to control their performance in a way that disrupts it. This control, which is often referred to as 'paralysis by analysis' stems from an overactive prefrontal cortex. One way to circumvent this type of paralysis is to **employ learning techniques that *minimize* reliance on working memory to begin with**." (Emphasis mine)

Sian Beilock, cognitive scientist[18]

---

[18] Beilock, Sian, Choke (Carlton, Victoria: Melbourne University Press, 2011), 60.

As a screen actor, you must contend with pressures inherent in the art and business of the acting world that render you vulnerable to the yammering of your inner critic. You must also commandeer those mental faculties that best meet your creative needs. Taking into account real-world labor conditions while paying mind to what science now tells us about ourselves, an optimal acting approach is likely to employ **nonanalytic learning techniques that minimize reliance on working memory.**

Sense-memory versus imagination

The great chasm between acting schools that use memory (e.g., Strasberg) or imagination (e.g., Adler) implies a greater distinction between imagination and memory than actually exists:

"Researchers have known for decades that memories are unreliable. They're particularly adjustable when actively recalled because at that point they're pulled out of a stable molecular state."

Science journalist *Virginia Hughes*[19]

Studies show that recalling a memory involves recreating it. The disparity between what we recall about events in our lives versus what really happened can be quite sobering. With sense-memory exercises, you are bringing up an emotionally impactful memory from your past. But while doing so, you overwrite the actual authentic memory by endowing it with the traits of your present acting exercise. The more you try to get meat out of the memory, the more it's stripped of its original poignancy. With overuse, you risk reaching back for your memory

---

[19] Hughes, Virginia, "How Scientists are Learning to Shape our Memory," Popular Science, www.popsci.com/article/science/how-scientists-are-learning-shape-our-memory?dom=tw&src=SOC, accessed July 6, 2014.

only to discover it's been turned into a tool. I question whether this un-witting subversion of our most meaningful memories—memories that form our identities—is why so many actors, including Stella Adler and Constantin Stanislavski, felt the Method was making actors neurotic. But that debate is irrelevant if neither imposing your own memories nor imagining your character's has any observable effect on-camera. By experimenting with the techniques outlined in this book, you will find yourself naturally gravitating away from time and energy wasting activities that do not translate on screen.

SCIENTIFIC PRINCIPLES
APPLIED TO ACTING

APPLYING scientific principles to acting allows you to unpack exactly what aspects of an approach work, versus what techniques may sound good but do not produce results on-camera.

"The moment you heard there was a Stanislavski method, everybody said 'well, I know the method, I know the method, I know the method.' And so in America it got very, very confused, and confused the actors, and was not as clear as taking a piano lesson, where you have to learn the keys, they don't change for anybody."

Stella Adler[20]

Correlation is not causation

Is great acting and career success **caused** by, or merely **correlated** with, acting training? The **correlation is not causation** principle used in science and statistics means that just because one thing followed another,

---

[20] Adler, Stella, in interview, "Stella Adler on the Stanislavski Method," YouTube.com video, posted by Orco Development, December 18, 2012, www.youtube.com/watch?v=LlvnBrE9wCI, accessed August 7, 2014.

doesn't mean that the first thing caused the other. In interviews, actors often talk passionately about their process, but on set you'll frequently find they aren't doing it.

"Stepping," key Makeup said as she stepped up into the trailer. Calling out "stepping" is a rule observed on set when anyone is stepping in or out of the makeup and hair trailer. The reason for this is that stepping in or out of a trailer causes the whole trailer to rebound for a moment on its wheels with the displacement of weight. The bump can cause makeup artists to smear eyeliner across the actor's face, or hair stylists to burn the actor with a curling iron. Everyone stops what they are doing for a beat when they hear "stepping." I looked over at another actress sitting in a salon chair facing the mirror that stretched the length of the RV. She had graduated from Juilliard, and I was asking her about her training and her process. We chatted most of the morning, as this film was a period piece, and it took many hours to get us in full regalia. Later that day when we were standing on our marks, I leaned in and asked her if she was doing the techniques she described earlier. She waved her hand and laughed, "No, no, I don't do any of that anymore." Just because an actor was trained with a particular method, and even espouses that method, doesn't mean their training is the root *cause* of their talent and accomplishments. Actors are unreliable narrators about their creative processes. Most likely this is because words and concepts can't fully capture it.

"Most of the great practitioners of the art of acting
know exactly what they're doing; even in the best,
most successful moments, when they let go of the

awareness of what they are doing, they still, somewhere deep inside their body, know what they're doing. There is a craft."

Meryl Streep[21]

Placebo effect: when belief makes it so

The placebo effect occurs when you do something you believe will benefit you and you experience the benefit because of your belief—but there's no real benefit in the thing itself. In so many fields, and none more so than acting, confidence plays a pivotal role. Feeling like you have a good handle on your craft can positively influence the outcome. In contrast, self-doubt can have a crippling effect on performance. An elegant theory can soothe an actor with confidence and confer a sense of mastery, even when nothing inherent in the theory itself can be shown to produce results on-camera. Aside from placebic confidence, it's sometimes tricky to determine if there's really anything of value within the approach itself; something that isn't merely correlated with talent but has a hand in helping you create great performances. If confidence were all that was required to be a great film actor, all actors could train at the "School of Placebo Effect," submit to the placebic delusion, and go on to have wonderful careers. Confidence may be necessary for your wellbeing and it can go a long way toward pacifying your inner critic. But that doesn't mean confidence is a sufficient condition for great performances. I've seen just as many bad confident actors as good confident actors. And some of the most memorable performances were those performed by an actor riddled with self-doubt. After wrapping principal photography on *The Accused*, Jodie Foster thought her performance so poor that she'd never work again. She went on to win best

---

[21] Streep, Meryl and Wendy Wasserstein, "Meryl Streep," Interview Magazine, www.interviewmagazine.com/film/meryl-streep#_, accessed July 6, 2014.

actress Oscar for that role. Paul Newman has said, "I started my career giving a clinic in bad acting..."[22] Kate Winslet came away from shooting *Sense and Sensibility* feeling like she had made a horrible mistake. Winslet too went on to be nominated for her role in that film.

Confidence is a conduit to mental health and happiness and has its value alleviating anxiety under pressure. But factors other than confidence are needed to generate strong performances. A danger of relying on an approach's placebo effect is that it is highly susceptible to doubt. If a single element of the approach fails in even the most minor way, doubt may creep in that can undo the placebo effect. If a placebo was pretty much all you were getting from the approach, in an instant you could be left with nothing.

Escalating irrational commitment

Escalating irrational commitment may arise from the **sunk-cost fallacy**, a principle used in psychology, business, politics, and military strategy. It describes the common human characteristic of staying the course even though there's likely a better way, because of how much you've already sunk into it. You have to ask yourself: is my course of study causing progress that the camera can see?

Confirmation bias

One of the tenets of science is to avoid **confirmation bias**—our psychological default tendency to seek out evidence that supports our views and beliefs and ignore evidence that might disprove them. An essential part of validating our beliefs is to try to disprove them. Applied to actors, this means you have to try the opposite of what *feels right*. Many of the experiments will feel wrong yet produce exciting results on-camera.

---

[22] Newman, Paul, "Newman Gets Animated for New Film." Reuters - TVNZ. June 7, 2006, accessed August 6, 2014.

The Camera: your teacher, best friend, and greatest collaborator

WITHIN a couple months of graduating university I was auditioning and working in films again, having effectively forgotten my acting training. I produced and performed in a short film, and my work was the strongest it had ever been. But since I was still running up against some of the same old acting problems I clung to the conventional notion that finding the right course of study rounds you out as an actor (escalating irrational commitment). This time though, another trek up the side of mount Sisyphus was averted by the acquisition of a video camera.

I started experimenting. My friends and I would prepare for auditions just as we normally would. Once we were ready, I'd film us running through our auditions. During playback we bore witness to how many of our choices were way off base. None of us were spared this realization. We did our homework and our choices felt honest and true. We were grounded in character and in the moment. The scene might play exceedingly well in the mirror or to another actor or coach, but when we recorded it and played it back, the choices didn't always work. The camera interprets human expression with a distinct perspective. Since the majority of auditions are on-camera, not checking in with the camera before showing up for our appointments was clearly putting us at a disadvantage.

In the early 2000s I was sitting in a small waiting room that smelled like pine air freshener mixed with new paint. Framed posters of the casts of TV shows graced the foyer. Folding chairs were lined up next to each other, each occupied by an actor or actress flipping through their sides[23] and running over the last of their lines with their lips moving slightly, or trying to relax by disappearing somewhere inside themselves. From just behind the door a voice invigorated by relief suddenly exclaimed, "Thank you!" A moment later the door opened and an actress skipped out, telling everyone to break a leg as she beat it for the parking lot. A woman came out of the office, checked the call sheet, looked up and said, "Sarah?" Sarah jumped to her feet, greeted the casting associate and followed her into the room, where stood a small camcorder on a tripod. I scanned those actors remaining in the lobby, recognizing most from this or that film or show, or other waiting rooms like this one. A tall actress arrived, flipped her freshly blown -out brunette hair, teetered over to the sign-in sheet in her four-inch heels, and exclaimed, "Good God, the traffic!" Everyone nodded. An actor in a smoking jacket, jeans, and Keds tried to assert his status by recounting how difficult it was to get to *all* his auditions that day. Another actor with the beginnings of a soul patch sprouting beneath his bottom lip made a quip to cut the tension that hung in the air. A second later we all sat uneasily, pretending not to pay any mind to the voices echoing clear as a bell through the paper-thin walls. Sarah spoke with the casting director about how much fun she was having recurring on a popular NBC show, then launched into an audition that made two-thirds of the actresses in the waiting room realize they'd misunderstood

---

[23] Sides are pages of a script given to actors for the purpose of auditioning.

the subtext of the scene. The other third either already understood the subtext, or still didn't.

My inner chatter reflected on an actor's turn at bat. One artistic swing. Athletes have targets to focus on, a clear objective. A means of measuring. A more perfect execution. But perfection isn't a goal for actors. Perfection is too clean. You swing, absent the focal point of a ball, allowing impulse to surprise even you. Sarah was still in the room. It must be going really well. A lot better than the actor before Sarah, who was in there less than two minutes and came out looking pretty dejected. Or maybe that was backward. Maybe the actor who was in there before Sarah nailed it and the casting director is trying to work with Sarah because she's physically right, if nothing else. Either way, in a moment Sarah will be walking past studio hangers, trying to find her car in a football-field-sized, blue-cement parking lot that looks like a massive dugout swimming pool, because when it's not used for actor parking, the studio floods it and blows at it with giant fans, creating a proxy for an angry sea during multi-million-dollar scenes with Tom Hanks. Then Sarah will have a careful conversation with her agent, "It went great…I think…What was the feedback?" Followed either by relief or defensiveness, while she assures her agent that it went well because she's a consummate professional, or that the poor feedback has some crazy explanation. In any case, she'll have no real idea, as casting was the only one who actually saw it.

Actors are told not to think about this. The host of reasons someone gets a callback or cast are too many and confusing to try to guess at. You must simply let it go. The audition process, an occupation of rejection, doesn't allow you to stand by your work. Nor does it give you the opportunity to gain insight from most of your mistakes, because you never see them. And your agent is even more removed. I didn't mind being vulnerable but I didn't care for being weak, and the entire situation seemed either deliberately or repercussively set up to keep actors suppliant. Actors who are great at auditioning aren't necessarily the best actors for the job either. Auditions are an entirely different beast. Neither actors nor casting directors consider the process ideal. I started daydreaming about a way to knock out prereads, and maybe even book jobs by simply submitting a prerecorded audition that could also serve as a visual-learning aid for feedback.

Instead of calling my agent as I walked past the studio hangers I called my father, a robot-building hobbyist from whom I inherited a love of technology. I explained my vision of setting up an online-audition-streaming platform and he was intrigued by the challenge. These were the days before YouTube–the video-sharing site came online in 2005. Flash had yet to emerge as a video-browser plug-in. Most videos were small, pixelated, and suffered from chronic buffering. In 2004 we managed to create the first online-audition videos that were clean and played smoothly.

It took a couple years for the platform to catch on. At first agents and managers in Los Angeles insisted no casting director would be interested. When I finally met an agent who thought it was cool and started using my online audition for pitching, casting directors paid attention. It was something they hadn't seen before and they were intrigued by the new technology, which has since been mainstreamed. Because it was new, they were forthcoming with suggestions to help refine and tailor the process.

Necessity begot self-reliance. Frequent filming meant even a reader became something to dispense with. I started using a piece of gaffer's tape stuck to the wall just off-camera as my eyeline. I'd then perform my audition, leaving dead space for the other character's dialogue, which I'd record later in GarageBand.[24] Once I'd recorded the other character's lines, I'd export them as a separate audio track and lay it into Final Cut Pro editing software. Export, upload, send. I'd always thought acting was a strictly social art form, but independence and isolation gave way to a new depth and fearlessness while experimenting on-camera.

---

[24] In the beginning I'd alter the octave of my voice in GarageBand when reading the other character's lines, but it soon because clear this was an unnecessary step. No one noticed or cared.

Working alone was suddenly both unavoidable and indispensable.[25]

"A classic study of musicians compared world-class performers with top amateurs. The researcher found the two groups were similar in every practice variable except one: the world-class performers spent five times as many hours practicing alone."

Daniel Coyle, author of *The Talent Code* [26]

Soon I was testing[27] for series out of my soundproofed, tungsten-lit walk-in closet, sending streaming auditions to the creators on location, getting notes, and making adjustments. A Showfax.com membership[28] allows downloads of twenty-four sides a day, so in-between auditions I worked on-camera with sides on the far outer reaches of my range, which got me called in for stuff against type. Auditioning for a variety of roles and getting feedback from everyone involved in the casting process, as well as feedback from the camera, allowed for a kind of training afforded screen actors in the 1930s and '40s who cut their teeth on B movies.

With this process I began spending a good deal of time behind the camera. An interest in directing developed as I filmed auditions for friends and then referrals, sharing with them the tips and tricks I'd been acquiring. I felt a profound allegiance toward actors who were bogged

---

[25] "Practicing alone is considered the single most important activity for improving violin performance." Ericsson, Krampe, and Tesch-Romer, "The Role of Deliberate Practice in the Acquisition of Expert Performance," Psychological Review, 1993

[26] Coyle, Daniel, The Little Book of Talent: 52 Tips for Improving Skills (New York: Bantam Books, 2012).

[27] "Testing" is short for "network test" and is the last step in the audition process when an actor is in the mix for a major role in a TV series.

[28] Showfax, a service offered by BreakdownsExpress.com, the official website where the bulk of casting notices are posted, allows actors in North America to download their sides for auditions.

down in the morass by vagaries and confusions between so many competing acting theories. I was sure what we do isn't rocket science, yet somehow science has managed with routine success to send rockets into space.

"While we teach, we learn."

Seneca, mid-first century AD[29]

The Camera and trust

You may be born with creative instincts that happen to translate on camera (i.e., you may be a "natural"), but to be a natural does not guarantee mastery. Even natural talents interested in expanding their range cross into unfamiliar territory. Whether you're honing instincts or developing new skills, appreciation for the camera's perspective on your work can only be cultivated by watching yourself on screen. This is routinely evidenced by how many actors stop themselves in the middle of their best take saying, "I'm just not feeling it." There are times when what you're feeling and what the camera's seeing will be in accord, but the frequency of this happening appears almost random, particularly in the beginning of on-camera training. Moreover, working on-camera offers objectivity that may become clouded if you are either completely new or have been mollified by success.

Almost everyone recoils when they first begin appraising their work on screen. It can take time to psychologically adjust to seeing yourself through the camera's eye, a perspective reversed and linearly removed from the experience of looking at your reflection in the mirror. I tell

---

[29] Seneca, Lucius Annaeus, and Sir Roger L'Estrange, *Senecas Morals by Way of Abstract. To Which Is Added, A Discourse under the Title of An After-Thought.* (London: Printed for T. Osborne, 1762).

actors to allow time for the emotional reaction. This is a part of adjusting your perspective. It will only take a handful of work sessions for the initial impact to wear off, and then you will be able to get down to work without distraction. At the other extreme, if you've achieved a fair amount of success as a screen actor, being able to see what the camera sees may present a challenge. There are many reasons for this, some more obvious than others, but a recent study out of Cornell University suggests more experience could lead to less rational assessments because of a reliance on a *feeling* of expertise.[30]

Of course, when talking about good and bad performance, we must grant that aesthetic preference will differ. When dealing with talented actors, however, these differences usually reflect style, not ability. If the actor is experiencing success blindness, I don't expect they'll trust me if they can't evaluate the quality of their work on-screen. So I'll ask them to bring a sibling, trusted friend, or significant other to be their reader during our work session. Those closest to the actor usually have no qualms bluntly offering something along the lines of, "Are you crazy? That sucked." At which point I can begin to unpack the details about what and how certain behaviors can be adjusted for the camera. Once adjustments are made, the actor is able to see the improvement by comparing the problematic take with the newly improved one.

Trust is earned

Actors are told they must "trust the work," "trust the process," "trust the director," "trust themselves." How many teachers have insisted you trust the work and then looked on like a disappointed parent when you failed them? Your inability to will yourself to trust is not a deficit. It's an asset for a thinking mind. It is the teacher's responsibility to earn your trust by showing that the work produces positive results. Trust is

---

[30] Nordqvist, Joseph, "Intelligence Agents More Likely to Make Irrational Decisions Compared to College Students," Medical News Today, July 10, 2013, www.medicalnewstoday.com/articles/263107.php, accessed March 7, 2014.

not part of the work, it's an effortless by-product that arises *from* the work, if the work is worth anything.

Three vulnerabilities of working without a camera

The experiments in this book are designed to reveal three vulnerabilities when working without the perspective of the camera.

1. Creative control

Actors already have very little control. Why give up more by putting yourself in a position where you're forced to take other people's word for your work? This is especially the case if others are assessing your work with their naked eyes and without the perspective of the camera.

2. Expert bias

At schools in Toronto, Los Angeles, and New York, I'd watch someone with fresh impulses get on a stage in front of a class and get coached into a worse performance. The instructor would say, "Great job," everyone would courteously applaud, and the actor would hop off the stage none the wiser. Putting your trust in someone else without your own ability to verify your work leaves you open to the logical fallacy of **arguing from authority**, or **expert bias.** Expert bias occurs when our brains stop judging situations rationally, after a perceived expert weighs in on the subject. Researchers in a PLOS One study discovered that the area of the brain that controls decision making had a marked decrease in activity when test subjects were given expert advice. The study's conclusion: "These results support the hypothesis that one effect of expert advice is to "offload"…decision options from the individual's brain."[31]

---

[31] Engelmann, Jan B., C. Monica Capra, Charles Noussair, and Gregory S. Berns, Expert Financial Advice Neurobiologically "Offloads" Financial Decision-Making under Risk, PLOS ONE, March 24, 2009, www.plosone.org/article/info%3Adoi%2F10.1371%2Fjournal.pone.0004957, accessed March 7, 2014.

Marilyn Monroe couldn't go anywhere without her acting coach Paula Strasberg, wife of Lee Strasberg, founder of the Method.[32] Fame afforded Monroe the luxury of bringing Paula everywhere she went—a total dependence that no doubt added to her deep insecurity, and a problem only money can buy. At any stage of your career, independence is the best investment.

3. Feeling versus seeing

We talked some about this third vulnerability when we discussed the scientific principle of confirmation bias. For actors it's our tendency to trust what feels right, the idea being that if it feels right it's good. Although actors work with emotions, your audience can't and won't care what you're feeling if it doesn't translate on screen. Screen acting is a visual medium. It's an art for an audience. The aim is not, as some treat it, therapy. First and foremost, what you feel must be transmitted visually in order to evoke a response in your audience. Yet actors are susceptible to overrating their own subjective experience when estimating the strength of their performance. If this admonition sounds counterintuitive it's because I am advocating trying what feels wrong. What feels right doesn't always work for the camera, and what feels wrong will often surprise you. How a performance feels is a risky yardstick for how it actually translates on screen, and ultimately, what emotions it stirs in your audience.

You may be just starting out, booking roles small enough that the director will not give you much direction or notice. Or you may be a series regular on a show where episodes have a rotation of directors and limited takes. In either case, you likely won't have the opportunity to build much of a relationship with your director. And you cannot rely on what feels right. You are flying blind unless you've developed a working relationship with the camera.

---

[32] Parker, Corey, "Paula Strasberg, Coaching Marilyn Monroe," memphisactor.blogspot.com/2012/12/paula-strasberg-coaching-marilyn-monroe.html, accessed July 6, 2014.

Working with a camera provides a system of checks and balances for you and your coach or director. Trust built on a mutual appraisal of your work allows for a more professionally constructive relationship both on and off-camera. The camera is an indispensable collaborator. I advocate embracing it and tailoring everything you do to it.

A place for analytic work

I have found the best time for analysis is when appraising your work during playback, making adjustments based on what you see on screen. Experiment, analyze, experiment, analyze, rinse, repeat. Yet this is not verbal, conceptual, intellectual, abstract analysis. It is visual, auditory, physical analysis. I have heavy doubts about how much, if any, traditional analytic work actually translates on-camera when creating a character in a fictional story. Of course, some analytic work in the form of research is necessary in instances where you may be playing an historical figure with characteristics that have been documented and for which you will be held accountable in your portrayal. Or perhaps the character is fictional but exists within a particular culture, like the navy. A note taped in the casting office of NCIS reminds actors that if they are auditioning for any character in the navy they must be conscious of their posture: shoulders back, head up. This is when creating relies heavily on recreating, when elements of your performance are learned by observing navy personnel or reading the note in the lobby of the CBS casting offices.

Perhaps analytic work has its uses elsewhere too—if you factor in the rarely allotted time needed to process analytic work, to refine the analytic fuel into a serviceable means of inspiration. When you only have a day or so to prepare a role for an audition or last-minute booking, analytic work ignites your working memory to white-hot temperatures that must simmer to be used effectively. For this reason, especially when working with time constraints, I recommend keeping all necessary analytic work to the bare minimum. With a brain full of research it can be difficult to know how and what best informs your character until you've had time to process. With analytic work, more time helps you feel sure-footed. Less time may knock you off balance.

You may feel strongly that your analytic approach has worked for you. Yet you may still be curious how much of the approach, how much background and research, translates into anything tangible on-screen. The effectiveness of any element of any approach, analytic or otherwise, can always be tested for on-camera. Try it. Try something else. See what reads on-camera.

Cultivate your mind

The best way to make great creative use of your analytic mind: read. Read history, philosophy, science, etc. In particular, read narratives of any kind, screenplays, plays, short stories, poetry and novels. Actors need to read at the very least to understand the stories they are being inserted into. The joke goes, actor flips through script, "Bullshit... bullshit... bullshit... my line... bullshit... my line... bullshit... bullshit." A handful of techniques for actors emphasize reading. Stella Adler's is the first that comes to mind. You will become a better actor and deepen your intuitions about story and character by reading plays and novels. There isn't much need to overthink this directive. Absorb through osmosis. Enrich your brain through passive acquisition. Read.

TALENT

A definition of talent for screen actors

MOST actors claim they are talented because of a few great performances in their past. Yet if most actors claim talent because of a few great performances, it's more of a common characteristic than expertise. When do a few strong performances best fleeting greatness and take on the characteristic of exceptional talent for the screen actor?

People talk about great actors as having erased all indication of their own personalities to *become* their roles. The flip side is actors who are so themselves, so open, vulnerable, truthful, that they move us with such self-exposure and authentic charisma. Many stars receive accolades for playing themselves but often go out on a limb for "Oscar bait," that is, roles challenging enough to get the attention of the Academy.

Another criteria for talent applies to the auditioning actor. Actors who must audition are expected to consistently deliver strong on-camera auditions, regardless of how challenging the role thrown at the actor with only one night to prepare. A simple and comprehensive definition of "talent" for screen actors can be summed up as requiring:

1. **Breadth:** the ability to "play yourself" as well as a broad range of characters and genres.

2. **Consistency:** consistently delivering high-caliber auditions and on-screen performances.

Psychologist K. Anders Ericsson, and researchers/writers Matthew Syed, Malcolm T. Gladwell, Daniel Coyle, and many others in Amazon's growing section of books on meritocratic human excellence, have documented studies touting talent as something predicated (in part) on ten thousand hours of results-oriented practice.[33] One major caveat of this principle is that copious practice only leads to improvement if you have the ability **to measure and verify your results.**

With the approach outlined in this book, even a novice can develop expertise on-camera, mastering breadth and consistency. You can make great strides toward becoming a talented screen actor before ever booking a paying job.

Steps to cultivating talent

The protocol outlined in this book minimizes reliance on language, concepts, and working memory when preparing for a role by using techniques that rely on impulse, emotion, and intuition. These are **soft skills** for preparing a role for an audition or a job, that is, when you are being subjected to external pressures. **Hard skills**—skills that are technical and pull more from working memory—are used to master the mechanics of working on camera when you are experimenting on your own, that is, in the absence of external pressures. The hard skills form the underlying foundation that supports the soft skills, creative impulse, and strong intuitive on-camera work.

---

[33] Although practice is instrumental in cultivating talent, recent findings indicate practice alone is not the sole predictor. We will discuss the most esoteric criteria that underscore the definition of talent for actors in a later chapter of this book. The backlash to the ten-thousand-hours principle is documented in the article in Fast Company, "Scientists Debunk the Myth that 10,000 Hours of Practice Makes You an Expert, March 12, 2014, www.fastcodesign.com/3027564/asides/scientists-debunk-the-myth-that-10000-hours-of-practice-makes-you-an-expert, accessed March 12, 2014.

PART II

PREPARING THE ROLE

NATURALISM—PLAYING YOURSELF

"Today you are You, that is truer than true. There is no
one alive who is Youer than You."

Dr. Seuss[34]

FOR centuries prior to the advent of film, character acting was the
only kind of acting.[35] The trend was caricature acting and melodrama, something that enervated Russian actor Constantin Stanislavski
and impelled him to invent a new system for actors based on naturalism and psychology. It's no coincidence that a naturalistic acting style
started to gain popularity in the decades that followed the birth of
moving pictures. Film was a new medium where audiences could see
performers with such magnification it was almost like they could see
inside them. The close-up shot enabled audiences to detect micro
-movements of the face that revealed universal truths that each of us
is innately equipped to recognize both consciously and unconsciously.
Audiences were beginning to discover they craved a new, intimate
experience. The popularity of naturalism that eventually became the

[34] Seuss, Dr., Happy Birthday to You! (New York: Random House, 1959).
[35] Hornby, Richard, The End of Acting: a Radical View (New York: Applause Theatre Books, 1992).

modern standard in film suggests audiences wanted to see something exposed and vulnerable, an honesty that would allow them to observe the human condition void of the thinnest of veils. They wanted to see people take off the mask.

* * *

Author to Dr. Ekman: "You've discovered three thousand different facial expressions that reveal emotions?"

Dr. Ekman: "We are capable of making about ten thousand different expressions, of which only about three thousand have any relevance to emotion, of which in any emotional conversation you're likely to see less than a hundred of them. So it's a very large vocabulary, most of which isn't used. Much of the variations are variations in the strength of a particular part of an expression. So when these muscles contract they can produce a very big expression, but the expression can vary quite a lot. I also take a look at the symmetry. How balanced it is on the left and the right side of the face. And that can vary also. When the movement is put on deliberately it tends to be a bit asymmetric. As the emotion becomes more genuine, it becomes more symmetrical."

* * *

As Dr. Ekman explains, a large part of your brain is dedicated to decoding the facial expressions of other human beings. Humans display something called *left-gaze bias*. When looking at a human face, our eyes drift left to scan the right side of the person's face. This happens because the right side of a human face better expresses emotion. Even dogs, our interspecies companions, have evolved at our side to display left-gaze bias when looking at human faces.[36]

---

[36] Racca, Anaïs, Kun Guo, Kerstin Meints, and Daniel Mills, "Reading Faces: Differential Lateral Gaze Bias in Processing Canine and Human Facial Expressions in Dogs and 4-Year-Old Children," PLOS ONE, April 27, 2012, www.plosone.org/article/info%3Adoi%2F10.1371%2Fjournal.pone.0036076, accessed May 21, 2014.

Not only do audiences seek to decode what characters are truly feeling and thinking, but screen actors also function as avatars for audiences. Camera angles such as CU (close-ups) ECU (extreme close-ups), as well as over-the-shoulder and POV (point-of-view) shots allow audiences to slip into a character's perspective and peer into another's face without any of the psychological pressures of having to participate. Film is celebrated for granting audiences this penetrating and unparalleled experience.

The majority of roles you're likely to book require that you *play yourself*. This style of acting has become so ensconced that I've heard professionals insist it's the only kind of good acting. It's a postmodern performance style that is antistyle. It is widely encouraged in the current creative climate for a number of reasons. Most commonly, directors like to cast actors who *are* the character. It makes their job easier. It's a safer bet they can get the performance they need.

"Don't act, *be*."

Lee Strasberg[37]

Actors who frequently play themselves are widely considered to be inherently winsome personalities. They include Julia Roberts, Michael Cera, Bruce Willis, Sandra Bullock, Will Smith, Cameron Diaz, Owen Wilson, Woody Allen, Whoopi Goldberg, Vince Vaughn, Clint Eastwood, Jack Nicholson, Robert Downey Jr., and Marilyn Monroe to name a few. Audiences are drawn to these people. They want to see them in different situations, combating different sets of obstacles, and fans pay to see this as long as the actor keeps it up. "Stars tend to be defined by their immutability. John Wayne was always John Wayne.

---

[37] Hornby, Richard, The End of Acting: a Radical View (New York: Applause Theatre Books, 1992).

Cary Grant described the secret of star acting as becoming 'as familiar in people's lives as their favorite brand of tea or coffee.'"[38]

The style of naturalistic acting requires that you do no more and no less than exactly what you feel in the moment. This produces a perfect symmetry between what you are experiencing, thinking, and expressing. Similar to the bilateral symmetry Dr. Ekman speaks of when talking about the muscles of the face, human expression that directly reflects human experience imparts a symmetry that communicates honesty to your audience. This is honesty void of filters, buffers, and affect. It's an openness that endears the audience to the actor who sheds the pretenses or personas we come up against in everyday life. Most of our daily interactions are varying degrees of dishonesty—boilerplate answers to, "How are you?" posturing, defensiveness, trying to appear happy or successful, feigning interest, or holding your cards close to your chest. It's wearisome having to play and react off the protective layers used to sheath our vulnerabilities against the critical eyes of others. Opening up to your audience shows audacity in exposing yourself. Acting on your moment-to-moment impulse divests the tip of the conscious iceberg to the deepest, coldest waters of that figurative Freudian id.

It's easy to overthink anything to do with acting, and playing yourself is no exception. "How do we know who we are?" asks Richard Hornby in *The End of Acting*, a treatise that challenges the dominant style. "When a Strasbergian acting teacher demands that his student play himself on stage, he implies the self is a given, but is it?"[39]

Hornby's critique points to why so many analytic approaches get actors caught in their heads. I don't think anyone can give a comprehensive definition of who they are. Such a concept is certainly far from given.

---

[38] Macnab, Geoffrey, "The Madness of Daniel Day-Lewis—a Unique Method that has Led to a Deserved Third Oscar," the Independent, www.independent.co.uk/arts-entertainment/films/features/the -madness-of-daniel-daylewis—a-unique-method-that-has-led-to-a-deserved-third-oscar-8510704.html, accessed July 6, 2014.
[39] Ibid.

Yet in a nonconceptual sense we know exactly who we are, and others know us too. There is a consistent energy, a unity that can be recognized. It is a *youness*. I've never met an actor who couldn't understand *playing themselves* in terms of just *being*—of honoring impulse in the moment. The screenplay strips you of the analytic component of your identity replacing it with made-up past and present circumstances. What remains of yourself is an energy, emotions, physicality, impulse, and perhaps other elements that don't have names. As you follow the stage direction of the screenplay and speak the lines, playing yourself boils down to the energy and honest moment-to-moment impulse that breathes life into the script.

Honor everything. Deny nothing. Do not try. Do not push, trim, fluff, or suppress. Again, you simply must allow, experience, without imposing your will. Do not play your idea of how it should play. Just *be*. To simply be means to trust that you don't have to show the camera anything. It will find what it's looking for all on its own. The art of screen acting lies in something simple, honest, and largely nonanalytic. Yet due to such a lack of control in the business of acting, we exert control where we can—on the art itself, making it a lot more convoluted and taxing than it need be.

For actors who have trouble simply being, a side coaching is helpful: "You're showing. Just feel it." Anytime the actor's doing anything more than reacting to the impulse, I'll remind them. Reminders in real time allow you to course correct whenever you are doing anything more than just being. And it doesn't take long for being to be accepted and become habit.

If you're experiencing anxiety in the moment, honoring impulse means embracing, feeling, and expressing that impulse. The honesty is compelling and simultaneously defuses anxiety by allowing it. Playing yourself is akin to when you're completely alone, in private, at home, relaxed, feeling and being effortlessly in the moment. It's all this…in front of a camera. The challenge and bravery lie within that antipode.

Playing yourself has been taught for decades, and different schools have different ways of instilling this. At the school for the arts I attended as a child, we were drilled on being honest, honoring the impulse, doing no more or no less than what came up for us in the moment as we read through the pages of our script. It wasn't until I came out to Los Angeles that I met the champion of what he's termed the *being-state movement.* I highly recommend these books by Eric Morris (no relation): *No Acting Please*[40] and the workbook *Being and Doing*[41] that provide many stream-of-consciousness exercises to overcome any blocks to simply being. As I said, I have found minor side coaching is usually all that's required, but his exercises are also effective and fun.

Experiment with honoring impulse when preparing a role that involves naturalism or playing yourself.

---

[40] Morris, Eric, and Joan Hotchkis, No Acting, Please (Los Angeles, CA: Ermor Enterprises, 2002).

[41] Morris, Eric, Being & Doing: A Workbook for Actors (Los Angeles, CA: Ermor Enterprises, 1981).

Troubleshooting Naturalistic Acting

There are several impediments to naturalism that this next section addresses.

Being "small"

It is overly simplistic to talk about being big or small. Issues that often arise have to do with the actor's behavior being disproportionate to the underlying impulse. As we discussed, authenticity is determined by the natural balance or symmetry between what you're experiencing and what you're expressing. The camera picks up if anything's the slightest bit out of sync and broadcasts the imbalance for your audience, who will be disappointed that you shattered their suspension of disbelief.

That said, if the impulse is big, corresponding grandiosity can play just fine. Screen acting does not prohibit big movements. Consider Al Pacino in the Attica scene from *Dog Day Afternoon*. Largeness must simply be grounded in strong impulse as the camera catches when an actor colors even the slightest bit outside the line. You must also be aware of the parameters of the shot—whether large impulse and movement fits coherently inside the frame.

Although less may be more, being *small* does not mean small energy. Being relaxed does not mean low energy. There is often a misunderstanding in translation from the conceptual to the physical. When asked to be small, don't deflate. Like sticking a pin in a blow-up raft, don't exhale deeply and purge your energy, mumbling unintelligibly through barely parted teeth. Practice exhaling lightly while remaining alert, both mentally and physically.

The camera picks up physical energy. A friend of mine was describing laser eye surgery, where a laser is shot into your eye and ablates part of your cornea returning 20/20 vision. During the procedure the patient is asked to hold perfectly still and look straight ahead without the slightest movement while the laser eye surgeon shoots a white-hot laser into the patient's eye. Most people panic about having to hold so still. The thought "Must. Not. Move." can make it virtually impossible to restrain yourself. Yet, in the time it takes for the irritation of a particle of dust or a thought to hit your brain and send a signal to prime the muscles in your eyes that would allow a flicker of eye movement, the laser machine senses your body priming to move and shuts off. It detects the physiology that predicts a reflexive movement within fractions of a second. Although none of us are laser-eye-surgery machines, thousands of years of evolution have endowed us with the ability to detect priming, or absence of priming, of the muscles of the face and body. Yet another similarity between acting and the practice of meditation is that you must remain relaxed but alert. When a person's face and posture do not appear primed to react to external stimuli or internal thought, your performance flatlines and you lose your life. This is perhaps why it is commonly said that acting is reacting.

A well-known TV actress and I were running lines in a hotel room while on location in Washington State. She exhaled deeply and caught herself, saying it was a bad habit she was trying to correct. She had an urge to relax with a full exhale, and demonstrated how, with the deep exhale, she lost the life of her character.

Another friend of mine stopped by after an audition, flopped down in my papasan chair and lamented, "Ever notice sometimes you think you're being *real* but you're actually just boring?" I had indeed seen him deflate into boring when being *small* and *real* and I'd been guilty of it myself.

If you are finding you are boring and losing your life when being small on-camera, keep breathing but do not expel your energy by exhaling a deep breath. Keep some adrenalin in your body by not over -relaxing and over-exhaling. Adrenalin produces different degrees of tension in the body. Unless you are playing someone who is seriously impaired, some degree of tension in an actor makes them riveting to watch. Too much tension produces anxiety and can become painful to watch. It's best to aim for the adrenalin balance of *alertness*. Alertness is tension without anxiety. Adrenalin release happens along a physiological continuum. You must become a master observer and maestro of this continuum. We will talk more about this in coming chapters.

Tears and laughter

Tears

Intense dramatic scenes often call for tears. Even if braying sobs aren't explicitly stated in the stage direction, you might feel the flow of tears to be the most appropriate response to the circumstances of the script. Perhaps it's a scenario where your children or the love of your life have been murdered. Usually the writers come up with something spectacularly devastating. Even if the writing is really good, an artificial environment and repetitive takes make it difficult to reproduce tears. It's not a failing on your part as an actor. The more aware you are, the more engaged you are with the truth of the moment, the more challenging this becomes. Your natural being-state may not get you to this emotionally heightened place, and it's death to start trying.

Fortunately there are two physical cues that can defuse effort and leave you in the moment with authentic tears.

When a scene requires reaction to tragedy, the first stage of the five stages of grief is denial. The first stage of grief also happens to be the height of drama, more powerful than the tension released with the flow of tears. The onset of grief is often a protracted moment before the breaking point. It's a moment when the character is in shock, overwhelmed, and allowing the flow of tears would mean acknowledging the reality of the unspeakable. Denial may last a brief moment, though sometimes it forges on for excruciating durations. Denial is intense. Your audience holds their breath, imagining this moment happening to them, being horribly ill prepared for an emotional onslaught of this magnitude. The immediate reaction to the first stage of grief—denial —isn't a gush of tears. In fact, a reaction vacant of emotion often reads on camera as a state of shock so profound, a calm before the storm so quiet, that what comes next could rock us to the core. It brings your audience to a point of such empathy and compassion, we are likely to break down if you do. So don't give in to relief too easily. Do not encourage tears, *resist* them. Resistance reverse engineers a buildup of tears. Resistance is also the state a person naturally finds themselves when struggling with denial. Resisting an emotion fuels it, which is usually an unfortunate catch-22 for an actor, but in this case it's exactly what you need. Let the intensity build until you can barely hold back, then let the tears flow.

"I thought drama was when actors cried. But drama is when the audience cries."

Frank Capra[42]

Incidentally, this is also the key to playing "drunk." Drunks are usually trying to keep it together. Relax all the muscles in your face and body and resist looking and speaking like a drunk.

[42] Capra, Frank, quote, IMDB.com, n.d., www.imdb.com/name/nm0001008/bio?ref_=nm_dyk_qt_sm#quotes, accessed March 9, 2014.

A second, more mechanical way of triggering[43] the flow of tears is a method actors have used for years. Warning: in order to avoid being sued by someone who will undoubtedly figure out a way to hurt themselves with Vaporub®, I must advise you not to try this at home. Disclaimers aside, the method I'm about to describe has been used successfully by myself and thousands of screen actors for generations.

Dabbing the tiniest dot of Vicks® Vaporub® just below the tear ducts —*not in the eye, mind you, but just below*—brings on many of the physiological responses to sadness, including tears. Very real tears will flow freely down your face. Menthol is the same ingredient used by makeup artists on-set, blown through a needleless syringe stuffed with cotton to protect against a menthol crystal being shot into your eye. I've had a crystal bypass the cotton and land on my eye—an incredibly painful experience that required the services of medics. Safety with Vaporub® is not difficult for most who use the tiniest amount of the substance just below the eye. Beauty supplies for film professionals carry a menthol lipstick that is both portable and easily dabbed in the corners of the eyes.

The menthol method is generally used for recording auditions at home or actual jobs on-set, and is trickier in live audition situations with casting directors. Another warning about menthol: menthol isn't a switch you can turn off and on. You may not want to apply it in front of the casting director and you may not want to apply it before walking in the room or you'll look on the verge of mental collapse before a job interview.

Laughter

Another big challenge actors face is pulling off authentic laughter. Celeste Holm tells a story about shooting the 1949 film *All About Eve* with Bette Davis, for which both actresses were nominated for an Academy

---

[43] This trigger is actually "reverse engineering an emotional reaction" which means to work backward, breaking down or manipulating the physical elements of emotional expression in order to recreate expression and stimulate the emotion.

Award. Bette Davis was notoriously difficult to work with and had strained relations with the entire cast and crew. Davis and Holm were shooting a scene together near the end of the film where Holm was required to laugh—to burst out laughing and not let up. Holm was pulling it off through multiple takes. At one point Bette Davis turned to her co-star and, disgruntled, she muttered, "You can do that?...I can't do that." Director Joseph L. Mankiewicz overheard this and ordered repeat takes of Celeste Holm laughing to rub it in Bette Davis's face.[44]

The trick to authentic laughter when moving in for coverage[45] is to have someone on-set sit below frame and tickle your feet. As utterly absurd or contrived as this may sound, if you're even the slightest bit ticklish, this trick will evoke real, authentic laughter, ample peals of joy for your director to cut together in post.

Again, laughter derived from tickling is laughter derived from impulse in the moment, not from mental exertions. You can gum up your brain trying to psych yourself into a laugh, a counterfeit for the real thing, or you can use tricks to leave yourself wide open for impulse, inspiration, and reflexive laughter in every moment.

Saccades, fixation, and nictation: how the camera reads your thoughts

When you scan your surroundings visually, your eyes dance over objects, darting from one point of focus to another. As your eyes appraise an area with these little jumps, your mind is putting together a meaningful mental map of the outside world. Your eyes react to thoughts in much the same way they react to objects in your environment. When trying to string your thoughts together, your eyes **saccade**, which is the technical term for rapidly shifting from one point of focus to another.

---

[44] Mankiewicz, Joseph L. (Director), All About Eve, 20th Century Fox, 1950, DVD commentary.

[45] After you shoot the master, you will go in for coverage that includes all your medium shots, close-up (CU) and extreme-close-up (ECU) shots.

When your mind lands on a thought inside your head, your eyes land on an object in the outside world. Even though the object is in your field of view, you are not really seeing this object. That is, you are not paying attention to it. It is as if the object you are looking at when you are deep in thought is a visual surrogate for the thought inside your head. When you are trying to put together a string of several thoughts, your eyes shift between several objects in your environment, landing on them without paying attention to them, saccading and fixating for brief moments. When the ideas finally come together to form a larger, meaningful idea, your eyes are likely to **fixate** on a single external object for a somewhat longer beat. The muscles around your eyes contract slightly as you stare, deep in thought. This is a version of **perceptual blindness** called **cognitive capture**, as you stare at something, not really looking at it but focused instead on the thought inside your head. An increase in saccades and fixation durations indicate someone is immersed in thought.[46]

In addition to saccades and fixation, as you think you engage in **nictation**, the technical term for blinking. You only require between two and four blinks a minute to keep your eyes healthily lubricated yet we tend to blink up to twenty times per minute. Evidence suggests that you blink to release your attention on a thought.[47] Each time you blink you reset your mind to a default state so you can shift your attention from one thought to another. This is not the same as a nervous twitch where eyelids blink distractingly. Fifteen to twenty blinks per minute looks perfectly natural.

When an actor tries to recall an inner monologue or lines that have been committed to memory by rote, the actor often engages in conspicuously fewer saccades and less nictation. This is a subliminal give-away

---

[46] Vinter, Phil, "People with Shifty Eyes AREN'T Dishonest...they're just thinking hard," Mail Online, www.dailymail.co.uk/news/article-2171330/People-shifty-eyes-ARENT-dishonest–theyre-just -thinking-hard.html, accessed July 7, 2014.

[47] Nakano, Tamami, Makoto Kato, Yusuke Morito, Seishi Itoi, and Shigeru Kitazawa, "Blink-Related Momentary Activation of the Default Mode Network while Viewing Videos," Proceedings of the National Academy of Sciences of the United States, August 26, 2012, www.pnas.org/content/early/2012/12/19/1214804110.abstract?sid=9bd3b79a-ffdd-4057-8459-8be8d4a53bd1, accessed March 9, 2014.

that you have slipped into autopilot and the lines are not stemming from meaningful, spontaneous thoughts. When looking for a line and not for meaning, mechanical, autopilot performances, or performances that are too 'clean' often reveal a sluggish blink rate and fewer saccades during playback.

One way to refresh your performance is to make it 'dirty.' I.e., when trying to think of what you want to say, you might flutter your eyes or fiddle with something for a fleeting moment. You may utter small noises; soft sighs, an "ah" or "um." Dirtying up a scene, or making it coarse means taking the time to search for the words while engaging in subtle, flustered behaviors associated with thinking. These behaviors emerge when we are unable to retrieve certain thoughts or the right word choice instantaneously. The struggle reflexively produces saccades and nictation. It may be helpful to consider these little ripples of activity the run-off produced as the brain makes meaning. Peppering a scene with this kind of behavior is not a protracted act. It happens in the briefest of beats. It takes just a moment to touch on the words you were looking for, but that spec of mental lint breaks up an overly sanitized scene.

Saccades, fixation and nictation are processes that walk audiences up to the entryway of your thoughts, but bar complete access. Audiences can relate on such a profound, instinctual level while remaining separated by a chasm to the mystery steeled inside another's mind. Saccades, fixation and nictation gives your audience little glimmers of insight into your character's inner world by revealing the shape of unspoken thoughts while withholding the details, a tease that human nature finds irresistible.

"Cognitive psychologists now tell us that the brain
doesn't see the world as it is but instead creates a series
of mental models through a collection of aha!
moments, or moments of discovery."

Tom Wujec, Information designer[48]

To avoid an overly sanitized or stale scene in the first place, do not pre-determine any thoughts, inner monologue or subtext. Moments of discovery by definition cannot be previously known or rehearsed. Audiences cannot read your thoughts, but they can detect when meaning is being brewed behind your eyes and the discovery that follows. By allowing for whatever thoughts come up naturally, you allow meaning, which effortlessly produces saccades, fixation and nictation and innumerable bits and pieces of what it means to be human.

Looking versus seeing

We spend a lot of time looking at things and not actually seeing them because we are absorbed by the thoughts inside our own heads. It's common and perfectly natural. The transition from looking to actually seeing will frequently be indicated in screenplays. For example, an actor may be playing a character sitting at his desk at work, lost in thought. A coworker enters the scene. "Oh hi," his character says to the character who just entered, "I didn't see you there." At the same moment, it's not uncommon for the actor to do a small eyebrow jump, blink, or small double-take with the head or eyes to indicate he is now *seeing* this new character. This action is often a misinterpretation of subtle physiology. For the most part, actors are unaware they did anything that looks artificial until they see it during playback.

What frequently happens in life is that you're hanging out inside your head, thinking, your eyes are passively looking around, saccading from one external object to the next as you jump from one thought to another. Or you fixate on an object and "stare into space." Then someone

---

[48] Wujec, Tom, "3 Ways the Brain Creates Meaning," www.ted.com/talks/tom_wujec_on_3_ways_the_brain_creates_meaning#t-345306, accessed May 30, 2014.

enters your field of vision out of the corner of your eye, or perhaps they walk right up to you, and you look at them for a fraction of a second before *seeing* them. It isn't a little double-take or small, surprised jolt. It's a moment while you experience a visual reverse dissolve. Your attention is grabbed and your unfocused gaze sharpens into focus. It is phenomenally subtle and universally picked-up on. It's a mental and corneal adjustment. Practice this by looking directly at someone while getting distracted by a thought. After a few moments, come out of your thought and bring the person in front of you back into focus. Register them visually before speaking to them. On-camera, you must allow the briefest moment for the mental shift and the lenses of your eyes to sharpen form an unfocused gaze to a focused one.

The Kuleshov Effect

An actor collaborates with the camera, with the writer, director, and many other elements of a production, but the actor also collaborates with their audience. In the early 1900's Russian director Lev Kuleshov conducted a series of film experiments that demonstrate how audiences interpret a screen actor's performance.[49] He filmed actor Ivan Mosjoukine and intercut this footage with footage of a bowl of soup, a young girl in a coffin, and a beautiful woman lying seductively on a divan. Upon watching this footage, viewers described the profound sorrow Mosjoukine felt over the dead girl, his pensiveness over the soup, and his desire for the woman. Yet Kuleshov had used the same footage of Mosjoukine in each context. Watch this experiment in the reference section at www.TheScienceOfOnCameraActing.com. The dubbed *Kuleshov Effect* demonstrates the cognitive impact of editing as well as how audiences play an active, not passive role in the art of filmmaking. Your job is not to convey the precise details of your inner

---

[49] Kuleshov, Lev, "Kuleshov Effect" YouTube video, 0:45, posted by esteticaCC, March 10, 2009, www.youtube.com/watch?v=_gGl3LJ7vHc, accessed July 6, 2014.

world, but to convey that you have one. Let your audience actively participate by giving them the freedom and satisfaction of interpretation. Take the guesswork out of it and you'll bore them.

Tone and style

Tone

Other than the camera, the screen actor's biggest collaborators are the writer and director. They set the character in a certain place, with a particular mood and mental life manifest in words and actions that reflect the genre and tone of the project. Common genres include comedies, dramas, epics, horrors, fantasies, actions, sci-fi, westerns, and any combination of these. Within each genre are different tones, intensities, and styles. Genres and their tonal subcategories are things that aren't too frequently addressed with respect to character work and acting techniques, yet actors often run up against the challenge of not grasping and serving the musicality of the piece. Don't think missing the tone is the same thing as putting your own unique spin on it. You'll simply stick out as a bad actor, or at best, not a very perceptive one.

One example of tone is the multicamera, half-hour comedy. These shows are shot on a sound stage with a laugh track (*Seinfeld, Big Bang Theory*), and differ in style from single-camera, half-hour comedies (*Arrested Development, Curb Your Enthusiasm*). One reason for this difference is that multicams use medium shots almost exclusively. There aren't any close-ups, so the style is similar to working in theatre. Note: if the project is multicam, the dialogue in your sides will be double spaced. Dialogue is usually only double spaced in multicam scripts.

Scrubs producers shot an episode called "My Life in Four Cameras"[50] where they changed the *Scrubs* format from single-camera to multicamera. The style change is jarring. You can see contrasting clips of

---

[50] Bernstein, Adam (Director), "My Life in Four Cameras" Scrubs, YouTube, 22:40, posted by ABCTVONDEMAND, Jun 23, 2012 www.youtube.com/watch?v=4aNFrI7jpZI, accessed July 6, 2014.

the same show shot in two different formats and the acting style adjustments the cast made in the reference section of: www.TheScienceOfOnCameraActing.com.

Single-camera-serial comedies and dramas have numerous tones and styles. Film tones also differ in style and intensity. Think comedies like *Anchorman* versus *Annie Hall*. A large part of tone or style is determined by dialogue. The majority of material requires the actor breathe life into a character to lift the words off the page. An exception to this is if the material is incredibly ambitious and smart, if the ideas and language draw the spotlight. For the most part, these situations call for the actor to serve the words by simply delivering them clearly. Adding almost anything is likely to produce visible waste on-screen. This can frustrate actors wanting to match great writing with equally rich acting. Conceptually dense, clever, rapid-fire material makes it easy for physicality and emotion to become distracting, overwrought, and silly.

Ratcheting-down and simply delivering the dialogue with no muss or fuss in no way diminishes your contribution or responsibilities. It's no small task to be in complete service to intelligent dialogue. Great actors compliment great writing by not competing with it. Examples of smart, idea-driven dialogue are writers Aaron Sorkin and David Mamet. In his book *True and False*,[51] Mamet says actors must serve the dialogue and not think or do much else. Many actors were insulted by his edict but the prescription is exactly right when dealing with his style of writing. "Just say it"—the three most important words when experimenting with this type of material. Experiment with the Mamet technique with Mamet-caliber material. If for whatever reason you run into difficulty finding this material online, rent the films and write out the scenes to practice with.

---

[51] Mamet, David, True and False: Heresy and Common Sense for the Actor. (New York: Vintage Books, 1999).

Reality check

How many unknown actors do you see starring in Mamet films? Stars get first dibs on good writing. Until you reach a certain level of notoriety, the job is a lot more than simply speaking the words written on the page. It's mostly about compensating for less compelling writing. Much of your job is spent enhancing what's on the page—WITHOUT CHANGING ONE WORD. For auditions this cannot be emphasized enough, thus the egregious use of caps. In her article in the *Hollywood Journal*, "Committing the Ultimate Hollywood Sin,"[52] casting director Marci Liroff refers to this offense as…you guessed it. At least one of the people making the decision to hire you is the writer, who won't be pleased if you decide to take liberties with his or her words. Worse yet, many actors get clever and end up blurting out a line worse than the one on the page. You may be quite clever, particularly if you're a skilled improviser or comedian, and you may actually come up with a better line, but save it for your own project.

Making bad writing work with stellar acting skills means you'll stand out from the majority of actors who shrug off auditions saying, "There just wasn't much I could do with that material." Support for the writing usually comes in the form of a strong character. In just a moment we will discuss character in great detail.

Sometimes the writing is so bad you have to use the exact same technique used for great writing and *throw away the line* to make it work—that is, squash any weight or meaning, spit it out, move on. Throwing away a bad line, or even swallowing a cringe-worthy line by moving quickly and barely audibly past it, ushers your audience along without getting pulled out of the story, without arresting their attention or offending it. Conversely, throwing away a *great* line can draw your audience's attention in via the thought, "Did I just hear that right?" Forcing your audience to double back in their mind offers a rewarding

---

[52] Liroff, Marci, "Committing the Ultimate Hollywood Sin." Hollywood Journal. December 9, 2013, accessed August 8, 2014.

challenge as they risk missing a clever turn of phrase if they don't keep up. In either extreme, the same technique serves the writing.

The job of the writer is probably the single hardest job in all of production. To the credit of writers, it seems more and more great writing is making it to the screen. At the time of publication it is considered a golden age of television. We can encourage this trend by paying to see the good stuff, but until we reach an unmitigated utopia of the written word, unestablished actors must make the most of crumbs that fall from the table.

Once you have a good handle on this method, I urge you, as I do anyone I work with: practice with the worst sides you can find. Bad writing is everywhere and bad scripts are not hard to find. With practice you can pull off great performances with the dregs of the dregs. It's rewarding when, at last, you unearth the key that saves the piece and it all comes together. Consider it a challenge of making art within narrow creative parameters.

Stylized writing

Another type of tone and style as categorical as Shakespearean soliloquies is found in Quentin Tarantino films. Tarantino's smart dialogue is an exception to the rule, "Just say it." His writing has a poetry and a distinct rhythm. I like to use some of the bride's speeches from *Kill Bill*[53] as exercises for actresses. Most women find it daunting. Good actresses want to play the truth of the scene and are inclined to play it simple, to honor the words, but that usually falls flat.

If you're an actress, a great way to get a feel for the tone of many Tarantino-style heroines is to place your hands firmly on your hips, feet apart in a grounded stance, chin down, voice resonance lowered out of your head and into your chest. This arouses the powerful tone of so many of Tarantino's strong female archetypes. Assuming this posture

---

[53] Tarantino, Quentin (Director), Kill Bill. 2004. (New York, N.Y.: Miramax Home Entertainment, 2004).

while reading Tarantino's dialogue is an effective way of putting the tone of his style of writing in your body. For both Tarantino's men and women, there's a physical and tonal ease and swagger to many of his characters. They move and speak with such supreme confidence that a playfulness arises from their poise. Watch his films and experiment with these qualities.

"Imitation is not just the sincerest form of flattery—it's the sincerest form of learning."

George Bernard Shaw[54]

Experiment with stylized writing, as well as mimicry. Reenact roles exactly as the film's stars play them. Mimicry is one of our oldest and best-developed forms of learning, so much so that we evolved a class of cells called mirror neurons for just this task. As Michael Caine says, "You must always steal, but only from the best…Steal any trick that looks worthwhile…analyze how he or she did it, then pinch it, because you can be sure that they stole it…"[55]

"Originality is nothing but judicious imitation."

Voltaire[56]

Before auditioning for a television show, go online and watch an episode to get an understanding of the show's tone. If it's a film, watch clips from the writer's and director's previous work. Genres, tones, and styles are blending more and more, with lots of ambiguity creeping in, so get the nuances in your bones.

---

[54] Shaw, George Bernard, Good Reads Inc., 2014 www.goodreads.com/quotes/185935-imitation-is-not-just-the-sincerest-form-of-flattery–, accessed August 1st 2014.

[55] Caine, Michael (Director) Acting in Film, Tmw Media Group, 2007, DVD.

[56] Pagel, Mark, "Creativity, Like Evolution, Is Merely a Series of Thefts." Wired UK. March, 2014. www.wired.co.uk/magazine/archive/2014/03/ideas-bank/mark-pagel, accessed August 6, 2014.

Expositional roles

There are roles in film and TV that exist merely to impart information to the main characters or to move the story along. When such roles come along it is imperative you do not distract from the function of the role by trying to make it more than it is. Show casting that you recognize a character's place in a story. I was auditioning for a guest star role of a counselor in a television series, and the audition consisted of long speeches that imparted information to the two lead characters. The information was the crux of the story arc for that season. There was no character information in the script, nor breakdown, and I recognized immediately this was an expositional role. When I finished reading for the casting director, she stood up, clasped her hands and thanked me. I had accomplished nothing special, which was exactly why she was so pleased. She said she had been meeting with actors all day who were trying to make more out of this role and distracting from the story. Of course her praise didn't mean I got the part. Another actress who also understood expositional roles booked it.

CHARACTER AND COMEDY

MANY actors face two pervasive challenges: mastery of comedy as well as character work. As a screen actor, you will be called upon to create roles for dramas that are multilayered and often quite different from who you are in real life. You will also be asked to tackle comedy. In this section we will examine how a single technique addresses both of these challenges. With only slight variation on the "be yourself" approach, you will also master comedy and complex character work.

Character work

"If the actor is truly to play a role, character must not be given as an intellectual exercise."

Viola Spolin[57]

The *be yourself* approach works an awful lot, and it's great advice most of the time. The exception to this rule surfaces in instances where playing yourself just doesn't cut it. Certain roles require the embodiment of a character different in almost every respect from who you are—Cate Blanchett in *Blue Jasmine* or Philip Seymour Hoffman in

---

[57] Spolin, Viola, Improvisation for the Theater: a Handbook of Teaching and Directing Techniques (Evanston, Ill.: Northwestern University Press, 1963).

Capote. These characters have heightened perspectives, distinct personalities, and in portraying these roles, the actor's physical appearance often changes dramatically. You may also hear many acting teachers, casting directors, and acclaimed actors talk about how everything boils down to simplicity, truth, and emotional honesty, while audiences and critics laud actors for transformative roles. Many actors find themselves caught between two seemingly conflicting philosophies: do you play yourself and just *be*, or do you morph into a character completely different from yourself? And if a completely different character is called for, what's a reliable way to succeed at an extreme transformation and keep it rooted in truth?

Comedy

"A tragedy is a tragedy... Any fool with steady hands
and a working set of lungs can build up a house of
cards and then blow it down, but it takes a genius to
make people laugh."

Stephen King[58]

Memorable comedic characters have unusual worldviews, written with sharp specificity—Dianne Wiest in *Bullets Over Broadway* or John Goodman in *The Big Lebowski*. Some consider comedy a genre for naturals. Others claim that if you were born missing the comedic gene, comedy can be learned as a series of broken down and masterfully executed rules. You may be wondering how comedic skill can be acquired without analytic scrutiny, without dragging it through the gears of working memory.

---

[58] King, Stephen, Good Reads, Inc 2014. www.goodreads.com/quotes/23315-a-tragedy-is-a-tragedy -and-at-the-bottom-all, accessed August 1, 2014.

Early in my acting training I made a few observations about character work and comedy:

- The only schools that seem to focus on comedy and character work are improv academies, and these schools seem to cater to sketch comedy.
- Actors who are naturals at character work and comedy often don't reveal much about their process; either out of a need to protect the mysterious pipeline of inspiration, or because a nonverbal process can't be explored in the language-based format of an interview.
- Until you reach a certain level in your career, the bulk of comedic auditions are for fairly clumsy comedies. These projects require a distinct character perspective to leaven the humor.
- To gain mastery of the full spectrum of roles, and to be able to work with any kind of writing, an actor must master both character work and comedy.

Strewn across a chewed-up hardwood floor of a studio apartment in old Hollywood were eighty fortune-cookie-sized slips of paper, each one emblazoned with a single emotion written in Sharpie. These emotions were **primary, secondary,** and **tertiary** emotions.[59] The primary emotions—such as fear, happiness, and anger—are thought to be universal and inborn. The secondary and tertiary emotions—like ambition and indignation—are more cultural. After graduating university I began working as an actor again, but still lacked important skills. I was in need of a reliable means of staying centered and unshaken in auditions. I was also unaware of a technique for creating dynamic characters completely different from myself, and how to handle comedy. If you put a comedic scene in my hands I couldn't trust myself with it. Sometimes I'd be funny, but more often it fell flat, and I didn't understand what brought about either of these outcomes. What felt fraudulent to boot,

---

[59] Greenfeld, Liah, "Modern Emotions: Aspiration and Ambition," Psychology Today. www.psychologytoday.com/blog/the-modern-mind/201304/modern-emotions-aspiration-and-ambition, accessed July 7, 2014.

was that I'd learned rules to make the material sound like the genre of comedy without it necessarily being funny. So I returned to acting class, because it was the only thing that even vaguely promised a solution. I had decided to film all my acting homework and see if anything stuck out. In the midst of the 2006 heat wave I was sipping actor Kool -Aid laced with the quixotic advice of one of my acting teachers to work on emotions, feel them, express them, etc. After writing out a bunch of emotions, I turned on the camera and concentrated on one emotion at a time, revving up their intensity like the engine of a car and noting where the emotion resonated in my body.

A study published in the scientific journal *Proceedings of the National Academy of Sciences* looks at where in the human body people experience emotion.[60] There were over seven hundred participants. Most people feel anger resonating in their upper torso, head, and fists, while depression feels like a cooling-off of sensation all over the body. These findings were consistent across cultures.

You can participate in the experiment online by clicking on the link in the reference section of www.TheScienceOfOnCameraActing.com

Using audition scenes, I read through a set of sides on-camera, firing up one emotion and keeping it going throughout the entire scene. I read through the first page of a scene twelve times, trying twelve different emotions. I then hooked up the RCA cables to the TV, sat back on my couch with my dog and pressed play. For the first few seconds I was relieved to see that whatever emotion I had put into my body was playing authentically on screen. But it didn't take more than thirty seconds to see something else was happening. With each new emotion, as I allowed it to resonate without interruption, and sustained it throughout the page, a new character began to emerge. I watched as my body and my voice reacted to this emotion like a musical cue and surges of impulse flowed into some kind of polytonal score. Each sustained

---

[60] Aalto University, "How Emotions are Mapped in the Body," ScienceDaily. www.sciencedaily.com/releases/2013/12/131231094353.htm, accessed July 6, 2014.

A map of human emotion in the body. Study conducted by Lauri Nummenmaa and Human Emotion Systems Lab members at Aalto University Finland

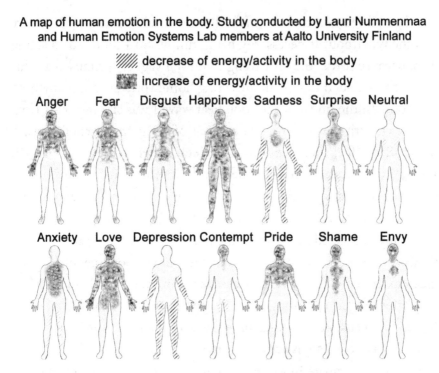

emotion, paired with the text, created a character as real as anything produced by the style of naturalism, but entirely unlike myself.

Sifting through a pile of scenes before landing on a comedy, I jumped in front of the camera to experiment. Sticking to a single emotion as a character throughline meant there was no need to map or plan. The single emotion was a lightning rod harnessing something I didn't have words for, other than it was working. I performed a scene repeatedly, and new, fresh, funny impulses would surface like a bubbling spring from depths so foreign and exciting it felt outside myself. By having this emotional anchor or focal point, suddenly other, much more creatively charged areas of my brain were unleashed and went feverishly to work. It was a shocking transformation. And paired with comedic material, either complementing or creating humor was effortless.

Something unexpected had stemmed from an attempt to solve a contrived emoting problem. I set aside any emotional blocks, spontaneously overcoming them, and began to experiment with character studies. What solidified the experience is that emotional throughlines could be faithfully relied upon as catalysts for comedy as well as complex character work, for myself and every actor I shared them with.

* * *

Dr. Ekman: "Some individuals have a particular emotion that dominates their life. It is the emotion that organizes a lot of their life, the emotion that they most often show, and that others know them by. One such person is the shy person, who's very apprehensive. Sometimes you can draw them out, but that's their personality. They are dominated by the emotion of fear. Some people are just hostile, and you keep away from them because they get angry so easily and so often about so many things and that's what they're known by. There are some people where the organizing emotion is disdain. They feel themselves superior to others and are somewhat arrogant in their nature. So there are a number of personalities where emotion plays a central, defining role. In a very well-adjusted person, context is going to be the sole or primary determinant. But in a person where a particular emotion dominates their life, like the shy person, or a disdainful person, then the context won't matter as much. What matters is their underlying emotion, which colors and distorts how they react to the situation."

Author: "Can the organizing emotion be positive too?"

Ekman: "Absolutely. There are people who are ebullient. They're in such a good mood all the time, and it's fun to be around them because they always see the positive side of things. They're cheerful people. So that's another personality, the cheerful person where enjoyable emotions are what dominate their personality."

* * *

Comedy requires the element of surprise. Watching a person have appropriate reactions, make appropriate decisions, decisions we ourselves would make when we are being most levelheaded, lacks any surprise. Nor is it very interesting. Watching someone with an original perspective, offbeat reactions, making unpredictable choices in keeping with the character's perspective is funny or interesting and frequently both. Audiences enjoy watching interesting and amusing characters move through the world, attempting to overcome inner or outer obstacles over the course of the story.

EMOTIONAL THROUGHLINES

EXPERIMENTATION distilled a list of emotions that can be relied upon to create great characters for the screen. I call them **emotional throughlines**. The emotions that appear on the right side of the less-than sign (<) indicate similar emotions of increasing intensity.

Admiration < Reverence

Ambition

Anticipation/Expectation

Assuredness/Confidence

Boredom/Weariness

Contempt

Curiosity

Determination

Dread

Embarrassment < Humiliation

Exaltation

Fascination

Frustration < Exasperation

Hope

Impatient/irritated/annoyed

Indignation

Lust

Amazement

Anger < Rage < Seething Fury

Anxiety < Panic < Hysteria

Awe

Compassion

Courage/Bravery

Desperation

Disgust

Eagerness/Enthusiasm < Elation

Envy/Jealousy

Expectation

Fear < Terror

Guilt

Horror

Indifference/Apathy

Joy

Mischievousness

Pride	Regret/Remorse
Revenge	Sadness < Grief/Despair
Serenity	Shame
Shock	Smugness/Superiority
Stoicism	Suspicion
Wonder	

On their surface, emotional throughlines may seem callow or two-dimensional. But they function as a sort of skeleton key unlocking aquifers of impulse. With this method there are three variables: actor, material, and throughline. Thousands of hours of experimentation proved again and again that any combination of the three produces vastly varying results:

- The same throughline paired with the same actor and two different scripts produced two distinct characters.
- Two different actors using the same script and the same throughline produced two completely different characters.
- Two different throughlines paired with the same actor and the same set of sides produced two dramatically different characters.

Change one of the three variables and everything changes. This simple formula produces the opposite of anything simple or formulaic. There are some key principles in working with emotional throughlines or character throughlines. The twenty-one principles we will be discussing are listed below.

Key principles

1. Try what can't possibly work

Although actors talk about taking risks, in reality, most actors resist trying what feels wrong. Of course, I'm not advocating you decide upon a throughline that feels counterintuitive and march into a casting office performing it for the first time, untested. You must push boundaries within the safety of a learning environment to discover what plays best on-camera. Your lab is where you must commit to what feels wrong. The only way to surprise yourself, grow, and improve is by knocking yourself pell-mell outside your comfort zone. Then watch what that looks like on-camera. Write numerous emotional throughlines on the back of your sides, turn on the camera and read through the first page of a scene with one emotion, for example, ambition. When you get to the bottom of the page, check off ambition, then start at the top and try contempt. Check it off, then start back at the top and try rage, then anxiety, then joy, and so on. Try any and all throughlines that strike your fancy, no matter how odd the pairing of the emotion with the text. During playback you'll see plainly within the first half page of dialogue which emotional throughlines work and which don't for a particular role.

A student once came to class with sides for a comedic feature film audition that was scheduled for the next morning. It was a character supporting role, a bellhop in a silly comedy. The script definitely fell into the category of mediocre to bad. So the job of the student was to bring the comedy to life, comedy that was only meekly suggested in the script. He experimented on-camera and the character proved amenable to a variety of different throughlines, but we settled on a favorite. The actor called me the next day to say that the audition went great. He committed to his throughline and got laughs. When finished the casting director said, "That was great, can you maybe try it another way?" The actor had about seven different emotional throughlines that worked for this role written on the back of his script from our on-camera session the night before. So he picked another throughline and read the scene again, committing to the new throughline. They loved it. When he was done, they wanted to see if he could do more. He knocked out five different throughlines, bringing five different characters to life one after another, delighting everyone watching. In the end, the movie fell apart financially, but the actor forged a great relationship with casting.

2. Once you've settled on a throughline, stick to it

Stick to one single emotional throughline as a character choice. Your character will still feel all their emotions, but stick to a single emotion as the character core influencing emotion. The temptation to vacillate between different throughlines throughout a scene or script never works. It creates schizophrenic characters. Literally, your character will come across as someone who suffers from schizophrenia. Actors place great value on range, but range needs to be rooted. Having range means having the ability to play a wide range of characters. Range is not the same thing as being emotionally disjointed. Being emotionally disjointed means fluctuating haphazardly between emotions while playing a single role. It is the throughline that keeps your audience identified with this person's story and perspective. Let go of your kaleidoscope of ideas and focus on your throughline. Keep coming back to it. The focus leads to a deeper understanding of character.

3. A character throughline only changes if it is the crux of the story

It's rare that anyone ever changes so dramatically that the only recognizable leftover is their physical appearance. Change this severe is so unusual and disconcerting it is often the marker of brain damage, multiple personality disorder, or an interpretation of alien or demonic possession.

Certainly people change. People mellow out as they get older or become even more eccentric. But we all have a temperament, a mood, an attitude, a core essence, an emotional energy that underscores our personality. This immutable element endures no matter how much our values, views, and demeanor may change over the course of our lives. Science has examined personality changes in lottery winners juxtaposed to victims of horrible accidents who are now in wheelchairs.

Within just a few months following life-changing events, people return to their general disposition. Those who were happy before the accident returned to being happy, and those who were miserable before the financial windfall returned to their state of discontentedness.[61]

When watching characters in film and television, observe how often they change and grow, their perspective shifting and evolving, yet there remains a character *essence*. A film that best exemplifies this is Charlie Kaufman and Michel Gondry's *Eternal Sunshine of a Spotless Mind*. (Spoiler alert) When Joel and Clementine (played by Jim Carrey and Kate Winslet) have important memories erased, they remain the same characters that the audience has identified with and cared for over the arc of the film. And the characters are still drawn to each other even though they have no memory of each other and may be doomed to make each other miserable all over again. Enduring character essences can be seen in many great films: *The Shawshank Redemption, Casablanca, The Silence of the Lambs, Chinatown, Winter's Bone,* and *Inside Llewellyn Davis*.

When a character evolves and their perspective and demeanor shift over a story arc, the changes are flavored by the underlying and constant emotional throughline. As an example, we like to see a curmudgeon fall in love. We enjoy observing how intense feelings of love, joy, and hope comingle and sometimes fight for supremacy over the character's surly disposition.

There are of course occasions where a character experiences a drastic personality shift that might necessitate adopting a new throughline. An example of this is Ebenezer Scrooge in Charles Dickens' *A Christmas Carol*. The one-hundred-and-eighty-degree character shift at the end drives the plot as the entire story is about a man changing from dark to light. Another example of a drastic personality change is the David Sumner character in the Sam Peckinpah film *Straw Dogs*. Sumner, an American academic staying with his wife in a quaint English

---

[61] Brickman, P., D. Coates, and R. Janoff-Bulman, "Lottery Winners and Accident Victims: is Happiness Relative?" Journal of Personality and Social Psychology, August 1978, www.ncbi.nlm.nih.gov/pubmed/690806, accessed March 9, 2014.

village, is taunted and tormented by the locals whom he fruitlessly tries to befriend. Eventually Sumner is forced to defend his home by killing a mob of locals so that he and his wife can survive. The dramatic transformation tracks Sumner from a civilized, docile, nonconfrontational, and reflective man to a brutish, desperate, primal animal.

Another example of complete character change is Walter White on the AMC series *Breaking Bad*. Over the course of five seasons Walter goes through the transformation from cancer patient, high-school chemistry teacher and father to drug kingpin. The show is *about* this transformation. The expression "changing hats" is taken literally as he wears a trademark hat as his new self and goes by a new name, Heisenberg.

When a character's core essence changes it is usually because their life depends on it, it is often disturbing or the crux of the story. Changing a character's emotional throughline is something that should be done only if there is a clear need in the plot. Otherwise, most great characters, no matter how complex, begin and end the story with the same core essence, the same emotional throughline that they started with.

4. Once you've settled on a throughline, commit to it

Once you've chosen a throughline, you must thoroughly commit to feeling that throughline. One way to think of this is that if your throughline were your spouse, **sticking** to it would mean staying loyal and vowing not to stray, and **committing** would be infusing the marriage with passion.

To push this metaphor to its brink, experimenting with an unintuitive throughline is like sticking and committing to a marriage that feels doomed. Naturally, actors are apprehensive when I tell them to commit to an unintuitive throughline. They will often botch their attempt by reluctantly appeasing me. Actors will only *sort of* commit to the emotion, while being slightly detached and dispassionate, judging it in their heads, telling themselves it won't work. If you're going to experiment, experiment like a scientist. Try to disprove your own assumptions. Sticking and committing to the most unintuitive throughline often works beautifully on-camera, and the choices aren't obvious to boot.

5. Feel it. Never indicate. Don't push a throughline

Do not push artifice. Don't force the expression of the throughline. Simply amp up the emotion, feel it resonate in your body, keep coming back to the emotion, the single word, through the course of the scene and the entire script. It's no more complicated than honoring impulse. Feel the emotion and it will come out of your pores. You mustn't *indicate or show* anything. *Just feel it.* Let it reveal itself without effort. Trying to indicate the emotion in anyway produces dishonest, cringe-worthy results. The honesty of your experience will broadcast itself.

6. Let the throughline flavor the array of emotions dictated by the scene

Your character must evolve according to the script, as well as experience a full range of emotion; but the essence of the character endures. Think of your emotional throughline as the key ingredient in a recipe that mixes with all the other emotional ingredients to create new flavors. Emotions, whether enduring or fleeting, filter our perceptions, ignite our reactions, influence our opinions, and help form our worldview. An emotion that underscores your day-to-day existence adds a conviction of character. If your throughline is joy and another character insults you, joy will filter your impulse and reaction. You would not react *with* joy. Reacting with joy to the insult is no more credible than a bipolar backflip from joy to rage, unless your character is psychotic. If you're a naturally happy, joyous person, your reaction will most likely be on the spectrum of surprise and hurt. You may become temporarily besieged with confusion and sadness as you struggle to recenter yourself and get back to your nature. It is imperative you don't overthink this or try to control it. By committing to your emotional throughline your impulses will react intuitively, in keeping with the character. Focus on your throughline, on that one word, and keep coming back to it as you make your way through the text. The throughline takes care of everything. Your character spontaneously reacts in ways that are always exciting and surprising but grounded in a strong identity.

7. Your throughline is a mantra

This method is simple but challenging at first, just as the simplicity of meditation is to the undisciplined and overactive mind. Like meditation, your mind will ache to do more. You may feel guilty, like you're cheating by not diving into research, writing background stories and subtext, breaking down the beats and thinking seriously about objective, superobjective, obstacles, etc. Your monkey mind is usually driven by a powerful urge to build a fortress only to knock it down; or as actors are often directed, to do the work and then forget the work. It may not be immediately obvious that the work is in fact a larger and more rewarding challenge: to commit to a creative meditation, resisting all temptation to make it more than it is.

8. Experiment with intensity

Although you must not push the expression of an emotional throughline, you can increase its intensity. Screen actors are inclined to be small, but if the emotion is honest and the intensity heightened, it can provoke big, thrilling responses that will surprise you and will read as honest on-camera—because it is. Always try ratcheting up the intensity of the emotion when experimenting. Conversely, experiment with the throughline resonating in your body in subtle ways. Sometimes the emotion will barely show. It can be a sliver of an expression resulting from a low-intensity throughline coursing through your body. If your throughline is *anxiety*, different levels, from reserved, low-level anxiety to panic will need to be explored. Again, don't try to *show* the level of intensity—experiment with *feeling* it in degrees. The expression of emotion, whatever the intensity, will always take care of itself. Intensity can have far-flung implications for character. For instance, rage usually lends itself to humor when it's reactive, sudden rage—when the intensity is so abrupt it overwrites any attempt at filtering. Rage plus the factor of time eliminates surprise and is often more of a menacing, plotting, seething rage.

9. Your character is oblivious to the comedy

"The way I approach comedy, is you have to commit to everything as if it's a dramatic role, meaning you play it straight."

Will Ferrell[62]

Commit to playing it straight. You're not *in* on the joke. Never laugh at your own jokes. You laugh and your audience won't. Your character might be smart (Lena Dunham in *Girls*, the guys in *Big Bang Theory*), just not so clever they're aware they're being funny. *Your character must be oblivious to the comedy.* Behave with the sincerity of a drama. However, you would not play a dramatic role with such solemnity it becomes melodrama (unless this is a stylistic choice of the director). Likewise, many actors working on comedy try to prevent themselves from smiling and breaking character by pasting an acerbic look on their face. This betrayal of commitment, a self-conscious Band-Aid, is often conceded by the subtlest tension in the corners of the mouth. The *tell* is the muscles priming for a smile, contradicting the stern facial expression. The

---

[62] Ferrell, Will, and Paul Fischer, "Will Ferrell - Cranky Critic® StarTalk - Movie Star Interviews." Will Ferrell - Cranky Critic® StarTalk - Movie Star Interviews, accessed August 6, 2014.

sweet spot is an unceremonious obliviousness, and the easiest way to accomplish this is to focus and commit to your emotional throughline.

10. The comedy is in the character

Comedy is said to have a shelf life. You've likely been unable to summon more than a painful smile and sense of history or nostalgia while watching older, joke-driven comedies with a succession of setups and punchlines. Jokes are often comments on a particular time, cultural perspective, and way of thinking. Later generations will not have the same frame of reference necessary to experience the humor. Another reason, of course, is that once you've heard the joke, the element of surprise that is crucial to experiencing humor is gone. With character -driven comedies however, the character isn't trying to make an audience laugh with jokes. For the character, the story is a drama. The comedy is a result of the character living truthfully and without irony. For joke-driven comedies, actors traditionally map out the beats, setups and delivery of each joke. In character-driven comedies, you can handle any new script pages thrown at you at the last minute because committing to the character leads to a plethora of ways you could deliver the lines in the moment. Even joke-driven, broad comedies benefit from a comedically rich character that allows the actor to forgo the analytic breakdown of the jokes and keep out of their head. Comedies are traditionally overlooked during award season. I wonder if this is because jokes sometimes supersede a rich comedic character in joke -driven comedies. When a fleshed-out comedic character takes the spotlight, richness and comedic longevity are the actor's legacy.

11. Playing annoying or obnoxious characters

One of the most important notes for an actor playing an annoying or obnoxious character is to remember that the character invokes those feelings in other characters, not in the audience. The audience must love watching the unpleasant character grating the nerves of everyone in the story. The distinction is that the character should *not* be insufferable to watch. Allow your audience that degree of removal. Be aware of this when settling on a throughline and any other character choice for an obnoxious role. Think of Pete Campbell played by Vincent Kartheiser in *Mad Men*, Maggie Smith as Violet Crawley in *Downton Abbey*, Hugh Laurie as the title role in *House*, Elizabeth Perkins as Celia Hodes in *Weeds*, Jack Nicholson as Melvin Udall *in As Good As It Gets*, and Reese Witherspoon who played the wonderfully annoying Tracy Flick in *Election*. Annoying and obnoxious characters are immensely entertaining, as long as they don't annoy their audience.

12. When comedic delivery is planned

If there is a specific comedic delivery you're aiming for with a line, decide on it but don't plan on it. Once you have an inkling of how you'd like to deliver it, shelve it in the recesses of your brain away from working memory. Don't get ready for it while you are performing. Do not anticipate it at any time leading up to the delivery. The anticipation will show and will undermine your delivery. Shelve the plan so that procedural memory may offer it up in the moment. If this does not happen, go with whatever impulse surfaces instead.

13. Scripted comedy = text + throughline + something unnamable

Something not yet fully defined happens when you apply emotional throughlines to comedic material. This something unnamable likely stems from the fact that the process is largely nonsemiotic. My advice, of course, is to simply experiment with it on-camera. What you see on the screen reveals more than anything I could possibly say about it.

14. Experiment with physicality

After settling on a throughline, allow for your character's physicality to surface organically. Committing to the throughline and the words on the page frees up your impulses to suggest how your body will hold itself while you become this person. Allow every impulse and see how it plays out on-camera. One actor with the emotional throughline curiosity was unaware that he was doing a very slight head bob as a non-verbal response to the lines from the other characters. It came across as a subtle gesture of unquestioning acceptance of what the other characters were saying. If the gesture had been translated into words, the unspoken idea was, "I hear you." What made it particularly interesting was the head bob preceded his chunk of dialogue that was written in disagreement with the other characters. His dialogue was assertive and intelligent and the most obvious choice might be to play the character aggressively. By maintaining the curiosity throughline, he was able to disagree with the other characters in the script while hearing them and challenging them with an understated sophistication that was borne from his throughline coupled with pointed dialogue. The sounds, gestures, and subtle reactions suggested the habituated tone of a human who had lived in this body for a lifetime. All these subtle nuances surfaced without effort or analysis and created a layered character. Yet all the actor was doing was committing to his throughline and the text. Implicit impulse guided the rest of his performance. Trust that your impulses know more than that voice inside your head.

Note: there is no rule that your character's physicality must surface via unconscious impulse. Although it has a tendency to happen that way, often you will enjoy experimenting on-camera and, through repetition, turn certain conscious physical choices into character habit. Experiment with mannerisms, speech patterns, physical rhythm and tempo, and so on. Experiment with conscious choices and allow for unconscious ones.

15. Experiment with voice

"Voice is…It's kind of the fingerprint of the soul."

Daniel Day-Lewis[63]

One evening I was coaching an actress auditioning to play a co-star role on a cable crime drama. The character was a stripper named Amber, and the scene involved her character speaking to the police detectives (played by the two lead actors on the show) who were questioning her about bruises and gashes on her face and body. Amber had been assaulted by the man they were trying to apprehend. We took a couple of minutes to experiment with several throughlines and settled on lust. When combined with the dialogue of her character and the circumstances of the scene, lust brought out changes in the actress's voice and conduct and colored an unconventional spin on her delivery. The actress's lines were peppered with details about perilous encounters with the culprit. Her dialogue also included questions about whether or not the officers thought they would apprehend him. The most obvious choice was to play Amber as though she feared for her safety. But the lust throughline transformed the actress's posture and slight physique into that of a confident, self-possessed adrenalin junkie, unwilling to be perceived as a victim, even when serious wounds and her own description of their relationship suggested she had been victimized. The most interesting impulse that arose out of the throughline was the raspy seductiveness of her voice. This actress had experimented with lust for other roles, but with this character there was a shift of tone and resonance that surfaced instinctively. The lust throughline, coupled with her physical and vocal transformation, added another layer to Amber that toyed with the meaning of her final line, delivered with a raspy curiosity, "Do you think he'll come back?" The effect was intriguing, and could have led to further development of her character or nothing more than an interesting delivery of information designed to move the story

[63] Day-Lewis, Daniel, quote, n.d., "First Look: Steven Spielberg, Daniel Day-Lewis and Sally Field," Oprah's Next Chapter," www.oprah.com/own-oprahs-next-chapter/How-Daniel-Day-Lewis-Found -Abraham-Lincolns-Voice-Video, accessed July 6, 2014.

along. In either case, the actress showed her chops. It was plain she could easily play the more obvious choice if requested, or larger roles down the line.

16. Don't feel a need to add on

Although many characters evolve from the throughline, it is important to recognize that sometimes a great character emerges in an instant. I'm still curious how this happens and speculate that by giving working memory as simple a task as possible, more powerful mechanisms of mind that operate beneath the surface of awareness are freed up to perform at full capacity. During playback you may conclude that the throughline is the only fuel your impulses need. When what you are doing on camera is great, no matter how simple the character's conception, don't cross the finish line and hurl yourself into the bleachers.

17. The throughline is a powerful tool for script analysis

Emotional throughlines are indispensable for script analysis, revealing meaning, subtext, and richness. With emotional throughlines, however, complex meanings buried in the script are revealed through discovery, not analysis. Many actors look at a page of dialogue unable to understand why the character would say any of the things written on the page. Once an emotional throughline befitting the character is found, the dialogue jumps off the page. The text suddenly makes sense, and a multidimensional character emerges, a character few actors would likely arrive at through analysis. One actress I coached was auditioning for a role in a film where she played a mother reacting to a car accident. A speech pattern she noticed in the dialogue, how she kept repeating herself, gave her a clue as to which emotional throughline might pair well with this character. While most actresses were playing the scene with the repetitive pleas growing more and more desperate (as heard through the walls in the waiting room) this actress chose the emotional throughline, shock. Shock is the disconcerting state where emotions aren't being processed because they are so disturbing they overwhelm the nervous system. Shock as a character throughline is often eerie and profound. The director told her that no one had understood how to play this role, and she got the part. At the time of publication, the film is yet to be released so I cannot give away the twist, but it turns out that the clue in the dialogue that prompted her choice of emotional throughline was more appropriate than she could have imagined at the time. This same actress auditioned for a film with sides from a scene in which she and her husband were hurling insults back and forth at each other across the dinner table. There are many choices you could make, but again, listening through the wall, most actresses were hurling the lines with venom and missing some of the subtext. The actress chose the throughline joy, playing it softly, and the love and dark playfulness between the dysfunctional couple emerged. Again, she got the part.

18. Character saves weak writing

Even if the lines seem out of place or awkwardly conceived, your emotional perspective will find a delivery that makes them work. I don't fully understand why this works as well as it does, only that it's endlessly entertaining to watch it happen.

19. Let the throughline be a jumping-off point

For roles where you have a fair amount of prep time, your emotional throughline may function as a jumping-off point that then fades into the background as your character evolves. There's nothing wrong with this. Again, all that matters is what produces great characters on screen.

20. It's not about the throughline

I often have to ask students to remind me during playback which throughline they were working with because I can't tell. This is also perfectly fine. Your audience isn't seeing your throughline. Your throughline works with impulse the same way light filters through a prism and breaks into colors.

21. Emotional throughlines are only one step removed from playing yourself

Your impulses are enough most of the time. They are enough because they are so much. Many mechanisms of mind are at work beneath the layer of explicit consciousness. A throughline, coupled with the material, is all you need to step into the flow, to create out of spontaneity, and surprise yourself during playback. It's deceptively simple, but when character is required for whatever genre, this method works better than anything I've seen.

"When you start to engage with your creative processes, it shakes up all your impulses, and they all kind of inform one another."

Jeff Bridges[64]

With playing yourself as well as with character work and comedy, the whole approach is conceptually basic: if the role calls for playing yourself, be honest and open, express no more or no less than what you feel and honor any impulse that arises. If the role calls for a character or comedy, use the same principles to stay true to your emotional throughline. Experiment with impulse, physicality, vocal range, and tone, but stay out of your head. The trick to discovering whether the material requires you play yourself or play a character is to try both on camera. The throughline is only slightly trickier than playing yourself in that you are

---

[64] Bridges, Jeff, and Philip Seymour Hoffman, "Jeff Bridges." Interview Magazine, July 1, 2004, www.maryellenmark.com/text/magazines/interview/907I-000-007.html, accessed August 6, 2014.

hanging out with a particular emotion, but the task is exceedingly simple when you commit to one word. After a very short time the process becomes streamlined as experience plants the approach in your bones. As simple as the process is, the technical proficiency acquired through working on-camera amounts to a long list of personalized mechanics that help enhance and finesse your screen presence. We will discuss this in Part Three.

Troubleshooting Comedy and Character

Can an actor play intelligence?

On a beautiful Sunday I sat in a cozy carpeted room with mismatched sofas and over forty students squeezed cross-legged onto any vacant square foot of cushion or carpet. The teacher called students two at a time to jump up and act out a scene we'd been instructed to prepare. The class was an intensive at a school with a comedy guru. The night before, I'd worked on my own at employing the school's method. But there was nothing funny in the terrifically unfunny, half-hour, multicam sitcom pages. The role was written for an ancillary female character, a beautiful woman who asks the sitcom's leading man, whom she's never met before, if he could help her because she doesn't know how to fix something mechanical. She then mentions that she and her lesbian roommate are massage therapists, and the guy is stunned at his good fortune…you get the idea. I followed the institute's instructions to the letter, but was having no luck evoking the magic I was told would come from the work. I wondered if anyone else was having difficulty.

Frustrated, I started working the scene on-camera using throughlines. Within three minutes I landed on *wonder* that inspired a subtle vocal rhythm, and it came together on screen.

The next day I sat on the floor squished between two actors. One actor after another performed this painful scene, and each time it fell to the level of the writing. The teacher pointed to me and another actor, and we got up and performed the scene. I stayed true to my emotional throughline. We were the only ones who got laughs. The material wasn't funny. The character's perspective is what's funny, and the character's perspective is why everyone was laughing. Adding the appropriate beats may work for certain well-crafted comedies with traditional setups and payoffs. But the jokes in traditional comedies have to be funny for these rules to work. If the writing isn't funny, rules about how to treat the writing may support the tone of the genre but they won't beget humor. I suddenly understood why comedy is largely considered something you're either born with or you're not. If you are a natural at comedy, your inborn comedic rhythm may serve to heighten well-written comedies and save poorly written ones. But if you are *not* a natural at comedy, scripted comedic training generally offers an understanding of the comedic form, but is less geared toward imbuing actors with comedic instincts. Yet all you need is to commit to a great character throughline. The choice is so distinctive you can be funny even if the material is not, while staying within or breaking form, and you can do all this without getting in your head. Comedy can always be found in the character.

The teacher, tone deaf to laughter, ripped my performance apart, dismissing it, then turned to the class and insisted it takes months of training at this school, breaking down beats and rules of comedy, to get the scene right. The lecture ended on a note chastising all the women in the class for playing the character with the assumption that she wasn't very bright.

That evening I mulled over the idea of how the role could have been played intelligently, if there is no indication of it in the script. Is it poise? Confidence? An alertness or curiosity? An air of snobbery? Articulation or a rapid speech pattern? Indeed, these are traits actors can use to support intelligent dialogue and intelligent choices inscribed in the text. I got in front of the camera again and tried various ways to play the role *intelligently*, but paired with text that lacked any suggestion of an above-average IQ, intelligent this character was not.

No attitude you put on can inform others of your IQ; emotional intelligence maybe, but not cognitive intelligence. Any definitive indication of cognitive intelligence to which your audience is privy is determined by the writer through the dialogue and choices in the script. The actor breathes emotional, physical, sensory life into the character. And this is the collaboration. I started noticing the collaboration breakdown in character descriptions for auditions:

ARLENE: 25–30, stylish, independent thinker, passionate, unusual beauty. She owns and operates the most popular restaurant on the promenade. She has her mother's brilliance and her father's shrewd business sense, but her passions lead her down many dangerous paths.

The actress is responsible for Arlene's physicality, her voice, and her emotional life, her passion, perhaps her lust, or curiosity, ambition or determination. The writer is responsible for character traits like independent thinker, brilliant mind, shrewd business sense, as these traits must be expressed in words and actions determined by the dialogue and plot.

✳ ✳ ✳

Dr. Ekman: "There are a number of other aspects to personality where emotion doesn't play a defining role."

Author: "I've been trying to narrow down exactly what aspects of a character's personality an actor is responsible for. It seems actor responsibilities are three-pronged: the character's physical appearance, voice, and emotional life. It strikes me that no one but the writer could possibly be responsible for the cognitive life of the character. Intellect can't be revealed without words/symbols [semiotics] and intelligent action in the form of dialogue and stage direction. We've seen proof of this historically. Until neuroimaging, patients who were unable to move and communicate beyond their primary physical needs were wrongly thought to be cognitively vegetative. Of course, the medical community now calls this horrifying state 'locked-in syndrome,' where someone may be alert and aware and their brain fully functioning, but they are trapped inside a paralyzed body, unable to communicate. I'm starting to think about how actor and writer collaborate to make up the fully functioning being, and I'm wondering whether you think this view in any way relates to how different mechanisms in the brain make up personality?"

Dr. Ekman: "Emotion plays an important role, but so does cognition, so does the way in which we have learned the habits of thinking that we have, our values, our conceptions. Even the language that we use only partially represents experience, and we often tend to only experience that part which is represented in language and miss other things. So emotion is certainly a very strong and important part of our personality and being, and of course especially so for the actor. But so is the way in which we appraise a situation, evaluate it, the beliefs that we bring to bear and the values that guide us, and none of that is emotional. That's all cognitive."

The universality of emotion

Dr. Ekman is perhaps most widely recognized for his work with micro expressions. However, another finding of Dr. Ekman's related to micro expressions is perhaps the most relevant to acting. Darwin theorized that many emotions are inborn and universal, and evidence supports his theory. Nevertheless, until Dr. Ekman's work in the early 1970s, the conventionally held view championed by Margaret Mead was that emotional expression was learned, and culturally dependent. Dr. Ekman's studies of preliterate tribes in Papua New Guinea finally proved that both feeling and expressing certain emotions are universal and unlearned characteristics of being human. He also discovered that recognizing emotions in the facial expressions of others is something we have evolved to do as naturally as breathing. Emotional recognition crosses race, gender, class, education, and geographic location. In other words feeling, expressing, and identifying primary emotions are not skills actors have to acquire. They are inborn. Although we aren't born with instincts for what translates on-camera we are born with instincts about feeling, expressing, and recognizing emotion.

"My job is usually to express emotion as freely as possible."

Meryl Streep[65]

Emotional blocks

Many actors have convinced themselves that emoting on cue is problematic. So much so that volumes of exercises have been developed to

---

[65] Streep, Meryl, and Graham Fuller, "Streep's Ahead." Interview Magazine, December 1, 1998. www.simplystreep.com/content/magazines/199812interview.html, accessed August 6, 2014.

coax emotions and relaxation. Yet such exercises reinforce the false assumption that feeling and expressing emotion are emulous skills. They make something we would do readily, something to achieve. Emotions become finicky the more we overthink or intellectualize emotional experience. In their natural state, emotions are spontaneous reactions. Treating them as a goal, a target, instead of a reflex objectifies them and delivers them to the domain of the analytic, a domain ill-equipped to deal with them.

One basic requirement is that actors are able to conjure an emotion on the spot. Any emotion. On the spot. My method for getting actors to do this is simply asking them to do this. The key is not letting actors think this is such a big request. I ask for it like I ask someone for a pen. And we move right along without the actor having a chance to think about it. You'd be floored how often this works.

Serious conditions such as traumatic brain injury, autism, psychopathy, or acute psychological trauma may inhibit a person's natural ability to feel, express or recognize emotion—and this is precisely why these are such serious conditions. Humans who do not live with these conditions have the full spectrum of emotions readily available to them. It's a huge, weird misconception that emotions cannot be easily called forth and effectively communicated between typical humans. In fact, the psychological sciences reject this premise yet the acting world still considers emotions these temperamental unicorns that live inside us and can only be indirectly lured. Coaxing a feeling (an emotion) does not mean faking an emotion. By its very definition, a feeling cannot be faked. Only the physical expression of a feeling can be faked, and that is rarely faked well.

I find the majority of emotional blocks are like a five-pound Pomeranian blocking a doorway. The earsplitting yapping may overwhelm your ears, but you don't need your ears to step over the Pomeranian. Your working memory can get completely overwhelmed trying to overcome an emotional block. But you don't need your working memory. In fact, you need to *stop* thinking about it. Rage is a classic example of an emotional block often seen in actresses, and it can be easily over-come. Socially, rage isn't ladylike or attractive. However, if an actress having difficulty expressing rage is asked to tense all her muscles, fur-row her brow, purse her lips, make a fist, and growl, rage comes. This is usually followed by a reaction of morbid self-consciousness. Some-times an actress will jut out her chin and her voice will become shrill when vocalizing anger. When this happens I work with her on rooting rage lower in the chest cavity. This takes it out of the head and gives it more weight and resonance. It also serves to lower chin and jaw, fre-quently giving way to a more impactful delivery. I want to be careful to avoid saying this is a "prettier" expression of rage. It is only an ex-pression more moving on-camera. Sometimes I simply ask the actress to mimic me. I lower my voice and growl, "Do it," and she does it. I smile, she smiles, we're all friends, and it's done. Although she may have reserved her doubts, once she sees the power and beauty of ex-pressing herself honestly on-camera, the self-consciousness dissipates on its own. I never ask actors for a figurative trust fall. All any actor need do is try it on-camera, and the truth is always revealed during playback. Although art is subjective, honest expression of emotion is universally compelling. The truth the camera sees is beautiful, even if it means the actor's face momentarily contorts in painful ways. Profound beauty is something almost everyone can grasp yet nevertheless evades a satisfying explanation. This is where the science stops, and the art of screen acting speaks for itself. If you are doing anything distractingly unappealing, experimentation and repetition allow you to finesse cer-tain behaviors into those that maintain their reflexive honesty but are less off-putting.

Reverse Engineering Emotion

REVERSE engineering an emotion means to work backward, breaking down or manipulating the physical elements of emotional expression in order to recreate expression and stimulate the emotion. For actors who are truly having difficulty experiencing and expressing certain emotions, Dr. Ekman has a method of reverse engineering emotions that can help get the actor out of their head and back in their body by making the movement so the emotion follows. However, Dr. Ekman's method is second in importance only to his observation that the emergence, expression, and recognition of primary (universal) emotions happen for human beings without effort. In fact, the repression of these emotions takes such effort that Dr. Ekman has a training program designed to detect when someone is trying to conceal how they really feel.

Dr. Ekman: "I developed the facial action coding system, the acronym for which is FACS. It's the first tool we've had for precisely describing different facial movements. And so I've given actors who are interested, a vocabulary. It's like musical notation for the face. You can hear music but if you want to be able to reproduce it again and again and recognize that same tune when it's played on a tuba or a violin, you want to look at the musical notation. My facial descriptive system provides you with that, and some actors find that very interesting. I've also worked with actors in terms of showing them how, instead of using a sense memory, they can follow Stanislavski's other instruction which is make the movement and the feeling will follow. And there are certain facial movements, if you make them voluntarily, it generates the entire physiology of emotion. And so I've taught them to use that as a skill to bring on an emotion when you want to have it as part of your performance."

Author: "In which of your books can actors learn about reverse engineering an emotion?"

Ekman: "Actors can look at the second edition of the book *What the Face Reveals*, edited by myself and Erika Rosenberg. It gives a very good description of exactly what FACS is."

Author: "Would you say then it's psychologically healthier for the actor to reverse engineer a distressful emotion rather than conjuring an upsetting memory from their past, via sense memory?"

Ekman: "I wouldn't say it's any healthier, but it's more precise. If we each remembered the saddest moment in our life, it would probably have a common characteristic of somebody dying, but who that person was and how old we were, and any guilt we felt about it, or any anger, it would be different one person from another. That brings in a whole texture of feelings, and the question of course is, how many of these [feelings] are relevant to the particular part you are playing. If you make the muscle movements of the face, that brings in the emotion free of all the associated memories, and anticipations and thoughts, and you can then choose what you want to add to it. It gives you the pure essence of the emotion itself."

Author: "Do you believe that if you experience an emotion, it has to be expressed somehow?"

Dr. Ekman: "The norm is, if you have an emotion, it produces involuntary changes in your face, in your vocal chords, in your skeletal musculature and posture. It's fairly quick and fairly inescapable. However, some people can deliberately succeed in hiding most of those signs and a few can hide all of those changes."

Author: "So if you weren't deliberately trying to suppress them they would likely manifest themselves?"

Ekman: "Oh, they would always manifest themselves. They're a crucial part of a package of changes that occur, and inform others [packages of changes] of which you are experiencing."

* * *

A study recently showed how scientists were able to successfully place false memories in a mouse. Memory "can be self-servingly Photoshopped, nudged off the mark by suggestion, and corrupted by being dragged out and rehashed."[66] Perhaps one day actors will be able to have false memories of their characters delivered directly to their brain. Until then, Dr. Ekman's facial action coding system for reverse engineering an emotion is a definitive remedy for actors who have, through trauma, social conditioning, or conscious mental effort, stilted their own reflexes. The codes for the action units (AU) give the muscular information needed to reverse engineer every conceivable facial expression; the physiology then triggers the emotion. Without explicit subversion, you cannot experience the physiology without the emotion, and vice versa. The order, for the purpose of acting, is irrelevant.

To determine if you are truly blocked, experiment with emotions in a nonpressured setting and allow them to come forward on their own, without mental effort. I recommend just sitting with the emotion, much like how you'd sit for a meditation. Notice where it begins to resonate in the body, how it feels physically. Practice allowing emotions to surface organically and know that you have Dr. Ekman's AUs to reverse engineer emotion should you need them. For the rare, entrenched emotional block, Stanislavski's final thoughts on acting championed reverse engineering emotion, or the *psycho-physical* approach. Dr. Ekman's work is the musical notation for Stanislavski's opus.

---

[66] Healy, Melissa, "Memories Can't Always be Trusted, Neuroscience Experiment Shows," Los Angeles Times, July 25, 2013, www.latimes.com/news/science/la-sci-implanted-memories -20130726,0,3603431.story, accessed March 9, 2014.

"My role in society, or any artist's or poet's role, is to try and express what we all feel. Not to tell people how to feel. Not as a preacher, not as a leader, but as a reflection of us all."

John Lennon[67]

---

[67] Lennon, John, "The Artwork of John Lennon." Exhibit - Fort Lauderdale, FL. Accessed August 6, 2014.

EMOTIONAL-INTENSITY SET POINTS

"We all boil at different degrees."

Ralph Waldo Emerson[68]

FRIENDS may describe you as someone who is enthusiastic and excitable. Or maybe those who know you are apt to characterize you as mellow and laid-back. Your **emotional-intensity set point** is where you are more likely to hover on the valence/arousal spectrum.[69] Our bodies have a set point for weight, a number on the scale our metabolism strives up or down to maintain. Similarly, we all have an emotional-intensity set point that falls somewhere on the spectrum of high (excitable) intensity and low (docile) intensity, or high arousal and low arousal of your nervous system.[70] An important note: your set point (physiological comfort zone) by no means prohibits you from experiencing the full spectrum of emotions and intensities. Our bodies simply tend to tip the scale in favor of one side or the other.

---

[68] Emerson, Ralph Waldo, Society and Solitude: Twelve Chapters (Boston: Fields, Osgood & Co., 1870).

[69] Andjelkovic, Ivana, "Brain Tag," UC Santa Barbara, n.d., mat.ucsb.edu/~ivana/200a/background.htm, accessed March 9, 2014.

[70] In this model, arousal doesn't mean sexual arousal, it means the level of intensity in which a person tends to experience their emotions.

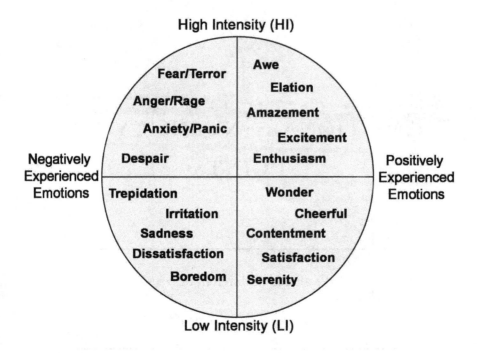

In this model emotions are not only categorized by whether they are experienced as positive or negative, but by how intensely they are experienced. Because of the different level of arousal between high and low -intensity emotions, it's easier to swing back and forth, left and right, on this scale than it is to go up or down. For instance, if you are some-one with a high-intensity set point (HI) you might readily experience a positive emotion like enthusiasm. In this excited state, it's easier for you to transition to another high-intensity emotion like anxiety, than it is to arrive at an emotion of lower intensity. If you're someone with a low -intensity set point (LI) it's easier for you to hover and transition be-tween low-intensity emotions (positive and negative) like serenity and sadness, or contentment and boredom. Actors typically display sets of behaviors based on their emotional-intensity set points, and both HI and LI set points have their advantages and challenges.

If you are an HI actor, you likely have substantial emotional torque, meaning you can quickly get to a state of heightened emotional arousal in a scene. The most common challenge for HI actors is the easy arousal of nervous energy. A later chapter addresses this issue in depth.

Another challenge for HI actors is sensing when to hold back. It requires a level of sophistication to recognize when a slow emotional build works better throughout a scene or entire act, or when a stiff upper lip is more moving than a full-blown emotional meltdown. Emotional torque isn't synonymous with good acting if the actor isn't creatively aware enough to govern it. When high-intensity emotions are over exercised, it's like a song that's all bridge and no verse.

The best way to get an idea about your emotional-intensity through-line is to gauge your nervousness at auditions. If you do not get nervous at auditions it is very likely you hover in the LI range. As someone who works in the emotional arts, being aware of your intensity set point lets you navigate your strengths and weaknesses.

Tension

Relaxation exercises are designed to release tension in the body, but a common misconception is when *anxiety* and *tension* are treated synonymously. Anxiety in the actor is undesirable, but tension in the body is neither good nor bad. Because everyone falls on different points along the intensity spectrum, different degrees of tension in the body work for different roles.

I work with an actress with effervescent energy and big, bright eyes. Even when she's sitting still, bored, checking her phone, her eyes remain alert and wide open. Her intensity set point is on the upper end of the spectrum. Her natural state is a state of great arousal, a state where she is most comfortable, and a state she settles into effortlessly. But for certain characters, it's too intense. She can practice relaxation exercises till the cows come home, but they can't change her physiology. Nor does relaxing help her play a low-key character, because her natural state of equilibrium is more intense than most.

When this actress is called upon to play someone with an LI set point, we have a cue: "half-mast." This cue triggers her upper eyelids, the levator palpebrae superioris muscles, to lower and she takes on the physical appearance of someone more laid-back. Though the action is small, the overall effect is transformative. For the vast majority of actors this cue would make them look weird, drowsy, and sedated, but for this actress, it softens her pertness. When working on certain characters, this simple movement has been her single most transformative adjustment. Due to her intensity set point, playing someone relaxed requires tension to maintain her eyes at "half-mast." A relaxed character comes across on-camera but could not be arrived at by the actress herself, relaxing.

On the other end of the spectrum are LIs. I want to be clear that high and low intensity set points are not value judgments, they are neither good nor bad. They are different intensities both with their advantages and challenges for performers. A challenge for LI actors can be putting tension in their body when the stakes are high. I can tell when these actors aren't fully feeling the intense emotion because the stakes are being expressed in their face but missing from their body. The camera picks up the disconnect making it impossible to believe them. When the pressure is on, our whole bodies go into fight or flight mode. The giveaway as to whether the character is truly feeling the intensity of the scene is most obvious in a close-up shot where the actor's neck meets their shoulders. When the body is tense, the trapezius, sternothyroid muscles, and scalene muscle group contract noticeably, creating pits and shadows in the neck, shoulders, and throat.

In a high-stakes scene, I'll often see an LI actor with their hand placed casually in their pocket just below frame. Or they may have one hip jutted out and are leaning to one side. LI actors in high-stakes scenes must take their hands out of their pockets, make two fists and tense up every muscle in their body. Clench hands, legs, butt, and whole body until they start to shake with anxiety tremors. This over -the-top tension shifts the body from their comfort zone to the higher end of the intensity spectrum. Once there, drop it down a notch so the shaking stops, while maintaining tension throughout the body. This

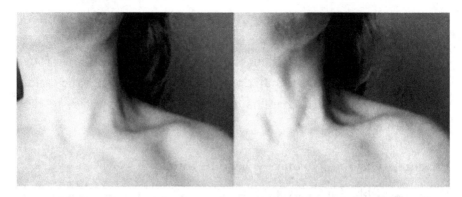

Photo left, shoulders are relaxed. Photo right, notice shadows and indentation, indicating tension and muscle contraction.

makes it easier to sustain and raise the stakes throughout the scene. Another factor is breathing. Actors often take a large breath in and exhale deeply before beginning a scene. In a high-stakes scene, you must tense your body to match the degree of tension called for by the stakes in the scene. Take a deep breath in and don't exhale deeply. Maintain shallow breathing until you hear "cut."

Although LI actors seem to be the minority in terms of the actor population on a whole, anecdotally I've noticed that the actors who work consistently seem to fall more frequently into this LI threshold.[71] LI actors certainly have the advantage of being able to keep their cool under pressure. Over the course of the day, actors enter and exit casting offices in rapid succession, each with varying degrees of anxiety. When HI actors flub a line, anxiety is more likely to creep in, an emotion that breeds discomfort in others. LI actors are more likely to brush off the flub and move on or laugh their way right back into the scene, having reset a more relaxed tone in the room.

One of the simplest ways for HI actors to achieve this kind of relaxed state is the common advice "just don't care" about the outcome of your auditions, a sort of actor nirvana few are able to reach and maintain

---

[71] I have not conducted a formal study so I want to emphasize that this observation is strictly anecdotal.

over the long haul. The lofty highs an actor gets from the intermittent rewards of screen acting raise the stakes and anxiety level. Getting to a point where you don't care about the outcome is the most direct route to achieve this kind of ease under pressure, but certainly not the easiest to acquire. Subsequent chapters outline a way for HI actors to ease anxiety under pressure.

Pressure, Tension, Dynamic—David Razowsky

I have never liked the pseudo dictum that all good drama is rooted in conflict. David Razowsky, a wonderful improv instructor for screen actors, coined the phrase "pressure, tension, dynamic." All great scenes have these three elements. An example of a scene with no conflict but with plenty of pressure, tension, and dynamic would be the type of scene where good friends are awkwardly trying to discern if the other has romantic ideas about them. Certainly if pressed, you could say the scene is about the character's inner conflict. At that point though, I'd say you're starting to do some heavy lifting to justify an expression better replaced with the dramatic requisite of *pressure, tension, dynamic.*

PART III

MECHANICS OF SCREEN ACTING

Cultivating Photogenia—A Face Sculpted by Habit

THE white, corded phone on the built-in by the fridge was ringing. I placed my tea on the table in the kitchenette and answered it. The unfamiliar voice on the other end of the line announced he was a police officer looking for a friend or relative of Roberta Morris. My mother had drifted happily out the door only a few hours earlier, kissing me on the head, saying she was going to go check out the Los Angeles Central Library downtown. Now the hairs on the back of my neck bristled as I told the officer I was her daughter.

My mom was on an escalator when she discovered she had epilepsy. The head trauma from her fall down the escalator, coupled with the repeated smacking of her head against the metal ridges, landed her at the University of Southern California's prestigious neurology teaching hospital where she remained for a few weeks, slipping in and out of consciousness and working through temporary retrograde amnesia.

I reached her with only the officer's brief recap of the incident, having no real idea what to expect. Under the bright florescent lights of the ER, my mom lay on a gurney, her head bandaged and bleeding. She was awake, her eyes fluttering, scanning the faces and beeping apparatus.

I caught her eye when she noticed someone pushing through the crowded ER making a beeline for her. She didn't ask who I was, but it was clear she didn't know. For sixteen years my mother had only ever looked at me with a handful of facial expressions, expressions children know well. I had become familiar with my mother's expressions of love, anger, impatience, devotion, surprise, sadness, and pride, but I'd never seen her look at me with confusion empty of any emotional connection.

A lot of strange things happen when someone close to you loses their memory. But the most perplexing thing wasn't that my mother didn't recognize me; it was that I didn't recognize her. Static things like her hair color and the lines in her face were the same as the day before, but every feature on her face looked like they belonged to someone else. Her eyes, ears, nose, cheeks, and chin were a different shape, relaxed, soft, like unsculpted clay. They moved differently. The muscles in her face had forgotten how to hold themselves. Over the next few weeks my mother's memories swirled back into her consciousness from wherever they'd been stopped up. For each new flood of memory, a corresponding muscle group in her face would shift and recalibrate back into position. After a month when almost all her memory had returned, her face was once again my mom's.

This is how I came to understand that through habit and repetition, sometimes conscious but mostly unconscious, we shape our faces over the course of our lives. I figured if we do it once passively, we can do it again with purpose.

"We are what we repeatedly do. Excellence, then, is not an act, but a habit."

Will Durant, summation of the works of Aristotle[72]

---

[72] Durant, Will, The Story of Philosophy: the Lives and Opinions of the Greater Philosophers (New York: Simon & Schuster, 1926).

Reprogramming habits

You've likely experienced how difficult it is to change a habit. The stubbornness of habit is also why habit can be so effectively relied upon. Once habits are formed they are so ingrained in our brain (basal ganglia), so immutably etched into our hardware, that we cannot erase them.[73] We can only reprogram them. In his book, *The Power of Habit*, Charles Duhigg offers a solution for overwriting habit that involves using the same cue and reward from the original habit while substituting a new, preferred routine.[74] For bad screen-acting habits, reprogramming is relatively straightforward when working with the camera. If the cue is "action" and the reward is a strong performance upon playback, adjustments to the routine are simply necessary to produce the reward. For this reason, I am suspicious of whether there are any screen-acting habits, the good and the bad, that haven't been intentionally created and cannot be easily overcome.

Many unwanted behaviors on-camera are more likely a product of not having watched yourself and applied conscious attention toward adjusting certain behaviors. Or perhaps the unwanted behavior is being repeated because it has become top of mind after you witnessed yourself doing it during playback. Whether changing an actual bad habit or simply paying attention to what the camera sees, the fix is usually pretty simple.

An actress once contacted me about her blinking problem. She claimed she blinked too much on camera. She couldn't help it. I filmed her. Sure enough, the blinking was distracting. She turned to me after playback and asked, "How do I stop that?"

I asked her, "Do you see yourself blinking?"

"Yes," she said, "It's as bad as I thought it was."

"So you don't like the way all that blinking reads on-camera?"

---

[73] Duhigg, Charles, The Power of Habit, April 17, 2012, charlesduhigg.com/flowchart-for-changing-habits/, accessed March 9, 2014.

[74] Duhigg, Charles, The Power of Habit: Why We Do what We Do in Life and Business (New York: Random House, 2012).

"No," she said.

"Then stop doing it."

She looked confused for a moment, then laughed. "That's it?"

"For many problems, that's pretty much it."

We continued to work on various other aspects of her on-camera performance and we never had to address the blinking again. With only rare exceptions, feedback from the camera is all you need to completely and permanently eradicate unwanted behavior and habituate desirable behaviors. These too can be reworked and made unconscious once again as needed. Again, adopting behaviors that appeal to the camera is not about vanity in this context. Although sometimes adjustments correlate with physical beauty, photogenia for the screen actor simply means conveying your art in a way that looks beautiful on-camera.

This next section offers general techniques for improving your rapport with the camera. Beyond these, the best way to truly improve your unique relationship with the camera is by dedicating the time to rehearse on camera and analyze during playback. This morning I read an obituary of the great "Tony Gwynn, Baseball Scientist."[75] Pro baseball players strike out an average of 18 percent of the time, but Gwynn's career average was only 4 percent. As author Jon Bois states, "Gwynn, whose nickname was Captain Video...had every single one of his plate appearances on videotape...He measured time in frames. Maybe he looked at his swing in frame five and was satisfied. If his shoulder was too low in frame seven, he would frown and go about the business of solving himself."[76]

Fear and Confidence On-Camera

A common problem that comes up for screen actors is the subtle (and sometimes not-so-subtle) leakage of anxiety or fear that creeps onto

---

[75] Bois, Jon, "Tony Gwynn, Baseball Scientist, has Died," SB Nation, June 16, 2014, www.sbnation.com/mlb/2014/6/16/5814622/tony-gwynn-died-hall-of-fame-padres, accessed June 16, 2014.

[76] Ibid.

your face under pressure.[77] Any number of things can cause this: frustration over how you feel the scene is going; distractions during a casting session or on-set; pressure from representation about booking; pressure from your landlord about overdue rent.

Fear itself is neither good nor bad. Its value depends on the context and whether it helps or handicaps. When the actor's nerves cannot be productively channeled into a role, it spurs the inner critic who interrupts the free flow of impulse. The first step in on-camera triage is prevention from hemorrhaging fear under pressure. Varying degrees of anxiety plague most actors, especially when it creeps past your immediate awareness unchecked. Many actors bolster themselves in an attempt to project confidence and protect themselves from the harsh appraisals actors endure. Unfortunately, bolstering can prevent you from seeing what everyone else sees. Like the cautionary tale of *The Emperor's New Clothes*, actors delude themselves into believing they are projecting their ornate self, when the truth is that on-camera you are naked. During playback actors who think they are projecting a cool self-image are frequently confronted with the painful truth, watching themselves display the telltale signs of fear that have bypassed their internal levees and trickled onto their faces.

* * *

Author: "Do you find it easier to detect the subtleties in facial expressions if you're a nonparticipant? If you are watching on a screen and not interacting with the person directly? Is it more difficult for a screen actor to pull off a convincing performance because the actor's audience is able to dedicate their attention to scrutinizing the face in close-up?"

Dr. Ekman: "Absolutely. If you're a participant, part of your mental energy is going into the task of figuring out: what did that person say? What did they really mean by it? And how should I respond? Other research I've done shows that people who know someone are much less

---

[77] Lerner, Harriet, "Fear vs. Anxiety, the Dance of Connection," Psychology Today, www.psychologytoday.com/blog/the-dance-connection/200910/fear-vs-anxiety, accessed July 7, 2014.

accurate in reading their macro or micro expressions because they have preconceptions and commitments. And they particularly don't want to see things that someone is trying to conceal from them, because if they are involved with that person as a friend, as a lover, they have a commitment to a certain view of them and they don't want to have it contradicted. So total strangers often see more than someone who knows the person quite well."

Author: "I've noticed, when an actor is trying to conceal an unwanted emotion, often a small muscle in one area of their face will contract, and for an extended period of time, throwing off the symmetry. With fear, it's a muscle group in the forehead that contracts and this one small movement is a major 'tell', throwing off the symmetry and making it quite challenging to believe them."

Dr. Ekman: "Yes, we call that a mini expression. It's a small expression, it need not be brief and it's usually in just one region of the face."

* * *

The camera sees everything and shares every detail with an audience that observes more going on in your face than those sitting right next to you who know you better than anyone. It's to be expected that the camera would induce varying degrees of anxiety in anyone who gets in its field of view. A nonanalytic approach is the strongest foundation for overcoming nervous tension on-camera. The next set of exercises goes the rest of the way in training your physiology against any indication of an actor straining to reach peak performance under pressure. A fundamental task in preparation for these next exercises is to expose your vulnerabilities to the light of day. Acknowledge and accept all. Use the Eric Morris exercises described in Part One to let impulse expose your true fears and insecurities. Confidence, real confidence, is just as much about earned respect and admiration as it is about full disclosure of those aspects of yourself that cause you the greatest fear, self-loathing, and shame. Real confidence does not have to fear exposure because you are hiding and denying nothing. You've emptied out. There is nothing left to expose. Real confidence is a quality the camera loves.

Some actors report that they do not feel anxious going into auditions. Some HI actors say they feel excitement instead of anxiety. Excitement, however, shares a heightened intensity with emotions like fear and anxiety. Again, it's much easier to switch from an excited state to an anxious state because of the corresponding intensity level. Once the intensity is in your body, you are primed for heightened responses, both desirable and undesirable. Heightened intensity progresses through increasingly stressful auditions, like reading for a venerated director or network testing for a series regular role on a television show where a sizeable quote is negotiated in advance. Situations like these are where your acting chops are put to the test, and a flickering asymmetry as you try to conceal self-doubt can inadvertently sway the confidence of those in a position to hire you.

Screen actors must learn how to control the asymmetry of nerves that appear involuntarily on their faces when slipping on a line or a crucial beat, or for whatever reason losing their center in an audition. The asymmetry appears as a clash of two emotions expressing themselves simultaneously while you try to believe the reality of the scene but also feel the reality of how the audition is going. The expression of anxiety or fear may be subtle, but the asymmetry as fear and confidence duke it out on your face is never subtle. More damaging than tripping on the line is the asymmetry of conflicting emotions flitting across your features. Any casual observer interprets the incongruity as bad acting.

If auditioning for a vulnerable role, or anything that requires that the character feel unsure, nervous, or insecure, then these conflicting emotions can be channeled beautifully into the character's internal conflict. If auditioning for anything else, this emotional leakage is likely problematic.

Two groups of facial muscles are at work when trying to mask fear. Because the actor's mouth is usually taken up with the task of delivering dialogue, actors seem able to control the lower half of their face, but the eyes and forehead will likely betray you. The contracting groups of muscles are the muscles around the eyes (orbicularis oculi) and forehead and brow (occipitofrontalis, corrugator supercilii), though we are going to focus on the muscles in the forehead. I have found that relaxing the muscles of the forehead triggers the relaxing of the muscles around the eyes.

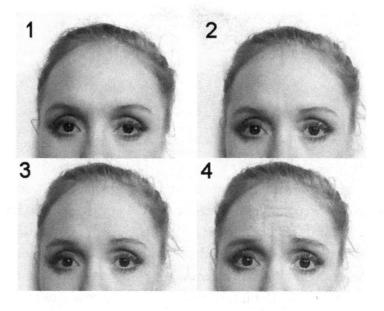

Figure 1 is neutral. The forehead and eyes are relaxed. In Figure 2 the forehead and muscles around the eyes are priming, beginning to contract and display the subtle leakage of nervousness. If you are trying to stay rooted in a confident character, an asymmetry emerges as your eyes begin to reveal the subtlest hint of vulnerability. Figure 3 shows a more advanced leakage of fear and anxiety. Figure 4 is an unrepressed expression of fear and anxiety.

An actor will usually exhibit a small level of leakage seen in figures 2 and 3. The subtle difference between Figure 1, 2, and 3 may seem almost imperceptible, but audiences watching your face blown up in high definition are exceedingly adept at detecting subtle indications of honest and dishonest behavior. An actor's ability to stay out of their head, both the analytic mind and the muscles of the forehead, is vital.

Some actors (especially those loathe to admit they're anxious) get so uncomfortable they're prone to eyebrow acting. This is terribly unsubtle and happens more often than you might imagine. It involves repetitive raising of the eyebrows as seen in Figure 5 below:

Making an unconscious habit of relaxing the forehead on command takes practice, repetition, and feedback. One of the best exercises I have found for this is placing the actor on a mark in front of the camera and having them wait patiently as I adjust the lighting and frame. Recreating certain on-set experiences to correspond to crew members tweaking last-minute technical details for a shot, recreates nervous triggers for actors as they await: "Action!"

Once I finish this adjustment, I tell the actor that my only expectation is that they be all right with making a painful mess of a performance on-camera. I then hand the actor a couple of scenes from a script and ask them to read for a role of someone with unwavering confidence. The scene has big speeches. I let the actor look it over maybe once or twice, but for the sake of this exercise the actor must cold read, reading a scene aloud and unrehearsed. I instruct the actor to commit to the character and to continue with the scene until I tell them to stop. The actor is given a chance to settle into character before launching in, usually quite convincingly for the first few seconds.

Before long the actor stumbles over a line, which gives them a little nudge from the confident center of the character. The trip up triggers the first sign of asymmetry in the eyes and forehead as the brow and muscles around the eyes contract slightly. At this juncture I tell them, "Keep going, but relax your forehead," and they do so while continuing to read. The next moment the asymmetry creeps back in and I repeat, "Relax your forehead." This can go on for much of the scene as the actor relaxes, launches back in, garbles the line, and reveals the classic asymmetric clash between the confident character and the self -conscious actor. With every trip up they struggle to keep the cool, breezy confidence of the character. I repeat the instruction making them aware of the physiology taking place in real time. If the forehead contraction still persists, I place my fingers gently on their brow to keep it from contracting as they read. The actor can feel when they are unconsciously expressing fear by noticing the pressure of resistance from my fingertips. This physical exercise helps make them aware of when they are breaking character and leaking nervousness. And it offers an outside-in way of controlling this.

Once finished, we play back the read. The feedback from watching reinforces the cues, and the actor very quickly internalizes the practice. It's simple, technical, and highly effective. While adopting this new habit, the conscious attention required to relax the forehead during stressful situations actually serves to distract the actor from the anxiety brought on by the situation. As we discussed in Part One, it's much easier to act when the analytic mind is occupied with a task.

As with the process of reverse engineering an emotion, when this habit is integrated and seeded in the unconscious, the relaxed forehead and eye muscles themselves trigger a more relaxed state. This allows the actor to commit more fully to the character, the environment, and the moment.

A few notes

1. Some actors grow indignant when interrupted in the middle of the scene to give an adjustment. Although being interrupted is never pleasant, if you want to correct a behavior it's most advantageous to catch it while it's happening.

2. A procedure popular in Hollywood at the time of publication needs to be addressed: there are advantages to making a habit of relaxing your forehead over freezing it with Botox injections. For one thing, if your forehead is frozen your eyes may still bulge, causing facial asymmetry. Secondly, it's quite a challenge to play vulnerable characters when you cannot express vulnerability with your forehead. Having the ability to express vulnerability while disabling unconscious forehead tension gives you more breadth and control.

The smell of fear

The smell of fear has always been a figure of speech, but new findings reveal that humans can, in fact, *smell* fear. The smell of fear is a pheromone that is secreted in our sweat. Although the smell of fear is registered unconsciously, it is easily transmitted in audition settings when you perform live and up close, and you are nervous. Casting directors and others in the room who are in close proximity to you inhale the pheromone that unconsciously triggers varying degrees of unease in them—an unpleasantness unconsciously associated with you.[78] Fear is one of the most important emotions an actor must work with. An antidote to transmitting nervous energy through visual cues or pheromones is to center yourself with confidence.

---

[78] Randerson, James, "You Really Can Smell Fear, Say Scientists," the Guardian, www.theguardian.com/science/2008/dec/04/smell-fear-research-pheromone, accessed July 7, 2014.

Confidence under pressure

Working as a screen actor takes impregnable nerve and what often comes across as a delusional degree of confidence to pull off over the long haul. Confidence is a great ally in the face of almost constant rejection. You may have heard that if you don't develop rhino skin you won't last in this business. But having a thin, translucent skin, being open and vulnerable, are the markers of actors who move audiences. You've likely also heard that you can't take rejection personally…but you're probably going to anyway. It's truly questionable whether you can be an artist and pick and choose what's going to affect you. You're putting your heart in it, your body's your canvas. You're being truthful, honest, being told to just "be yourself." And feedback often comes in the form of something unmistakably personal. Not taking rejection personally is just another task lobbed to your feeble working memory that it can't possibly handle. So many actors wind up feeling bad about the rejection and then feeling bad about feeling bad about the rejection.

Your self-image

Like a character backstory, you have your own backstory; a lifetime of memories that makes up a concept of who you are. This is called your **autobiographical memory base**. As the study "Memory and the Self" in the *Journal of Memory and Language* states, "Autobiographical knowledge constrains what the self is, has been, and can be."[79]

Memories of rejection are sewn into the fabric of your self-image, which in turn narrows the parameters of what you can accomplish. To make matters worse, biologically our brains have evolved to retain memories of negative experiences in order to avoid them, a self-preservation measure for survival and reproduction. Psychologists call this human characteristic **negativity bias**.[80] You are biologically primed to

---

[79] Conway, Martin A., "Memory and the Self," Journal of Memory and Language, October 2005, www.sciencedirect.com/science/article/pii/S0749596X05000987, accessed July 7, 2014.

[80] Marano, Hara Estroff, "Our Brain's Negative Bias," Psychology Today, www.psychologytoday.com/articles/200306/our-brains-negative-bias, accessed July 7, 2014.

incorporate more negative memories into your identity than positive ones. In the wild, negativity bias helps keep you alive so you can reproduce. In modern society, negativity bias can keep you from achieving goals that extend beyond the basics of survival and reproduction. Perhaps actors don't need an absurd degree of confidence as much as a more accurate balance between the good and bad memories that make up your self-image.

The following exercises train your brain to repopulate your identity with emotionally charged memories of past accomplishments, reinforcing your self-image against negativity bias. The resulting confidence helps you carry out stronger performances, which aids in achieving your goals. This is a self-perpetuating thought cycle to help foster success. I want to caution against equating a more positive identity with magical thinking. A positive disposition is attractive, emotions are infectious, and we want to be around those who make us feel good. A great deal of fortune in life, the good and the bad, whether you are aware of it or not, is determined by social influence. Yet popular schools of thought on positive thinking make claims that thought has almost supernatural powers to enhance prosperity. A recent article in the *New Yorker* cites several studies that show "fantasies hamper progress" [81] in some instances. In fact, the journal *Psychological Science* published a study in February 2014 titled "Positive Thinking about the Future in Newspaper Reports and Presidential Addresses Predicts Economic Downturn." The first sentence in the abstract reads: "Previous research has shown that positive thinking, in the form of fantasies about an idealized future, predicts low effort and poor performance."[82] Additionally, popular belief systems about positive thinking often ascribe blame to the victims of grave misfortune for not having positively thought

---

[81] Alter, Adam, "The Powerlessness of Positive Thinking," the New Yorker, www.newyorker.com/online/blogs/currency/2014/02/the-powerlessness-of-positive-thinking.html, accessed July 7, 2014.

[82] Sevincer, A.T., G. Wagner, J. Kalvelage, and G. Oettingen, "Positive Thinking about the Future in Newspaper Reports and Presidential Addresses Predicts Economic Downturn," Journal of the Association for Psychological Science, November 26, 2013, pss.sagepub.com/content/early/2014/02/04/0956797613518350.abstract, accessed March 9, 2014.

themselves into a better outcome. I have seen this distorted worldview isolate those most in need of compassion and support.

Therefore, it's safest to recognize thought as a yet-to-be fully un-packed mystery, and refrain from presumptive speculation or oversim-plification. Instead, I'd like to focus on a general appreciation for the power of thought. Observable facets of thought impact our emotions and physiology in complex yet tangible ways that play out in the so-cial strata that shape our lives. The upcoming exercises are designed to cultivate confidence. Magic would be great, but confidence on its own has a measurable payoff in the social order of human artistic expression and the business of entertainment.

Note: positive visualization exercises have been used for years by cognitive and sports psychologists. For those interested in an in-depth discussion of such exercises in a sports context, see *The Mental Edge* by Kenneth Baum.[83]

Exercise #1: positive identity

Reflect back on your past, jotting down as many memories as you're able to recall about times when you felt confident, poised, on your mark, on the ball, and in the zone. These memories don't necessarily have to pertain to acting. Get all your best acting memories down, but if you have memories from a sport, another art, discipline, or any other area of your life, write them down as well.

Once you have a list, set aside ten minutes, find a comfortable place to sit, relax, pick the memory furthest back, and start daydreaming. With your eyes closed, bring this memory back into your mind and crank up the sensorial and emotional volume on the memory making it especially vivid. Positive emotions are the key. The most important aspect of the daydream is to experience the positive emotions and sen-sations to their maximum intensity and then let them simmer inside

---

[83] Baum, Kenneth, The Mental Edge: Maximize your Sports Potential with the Mind-Body Connection (New York: Berkley Publishing Group, 1999).

you. When you wrap up this relived memory, make sure it ends on a positive feeling.

Go down your list of these memories and settle into a sensory and emotionally charged visualization for approximately ten minutes a day. In about two weeks your concept of self will have reintegrated these positive memories, lifting psychologically biased limitations and literally broadening your capabilities. After the two weeks, you may repeat this exercise as needed.

Exercise #2: immediate goals

The second phase of these exercises is something you do before auditions. If you do not have auditions lined up, imagine that you do and perform this exercise for your imagined auditions. Imagine yourself going through the entire process leading up to and through your audition. Maximize the senses as you imagine this audition going superbly and amplify the positive emotions associated with peak performance. As you leave the audition, rev up the feeling of having performed your best. Max out those positive feelings as you slip out of your visualization.

Not only do you not have to *believe* the visualization for it to be effective, you must stop yourself from *trying* to believe it. While making the visualization as vivid and emotionally charged as possible, resist every urge to try to convince yourself of the likelihood of this possible outcome. Don't let your working memory work too hard on your fantasy. Effort and pressure are counterproductive. Simply enjoy the visualization as you would a daydream. The power of a vivid daydream is not for working memory to muddle. The effect of a vivid visualization passively affixes itself inside your procedural memory. Procedural memory may then take this visualization as an unconscious directive.

I recommend doing the immediate goals exercise at least once a day for the first two weeks, then once a week or as needed for maintenance.

Positive memories and targeted visualizations allow your body to disassociate from memories of bad audition experiences. You will no longer unwittingly use past negative experiences that feed your negativity bias as guideposts for future auditions. It's simple but it takes discipline to commit to these exercises. They require a delicate hand and no pressure. They require repetition and consistency, even (and especially) if you're cynical about these types of exercises. Make note of new, positive experiences and do a visualization to fortify your connection to them. Anchor new success with your self-image.

Negative thoughts

As we discussed in Part One, ironic rebound is the phenomenon where unwanted thoughts come up with even more persistence and frequency the more unwanted they are. This is why actors who prepare for a role using a classic analytic method can run into yet another problem when they are instructed to "forget the work" for performance. In her book *The Willpower Instinct* (a book I highly recommend), Dr. Kelly McGonigal discusses some of the work of her colleague at Stanford University, Dr. Daniel Wagner.[84] Wagner is one of the scientists[85] who proffered the theory that thought suppression routinely fails because two different mechanisms of mind split the task "don't think about X." One part of our brain, **the operator,** uses a great deal of mental energy and effort looking for anything else to think about. Meanwhile, another part of our brain, **the monitor,** runs automatically and draws very little energy in its constant search for signs you might be feeling or thinking the forbidden thought or feeling. As you might imagine, pressure in performance and audition settings risks overtaxing the mental energy required for the operator to function. When the operator is exhausted you're left with an unchecked monitor running on autopilot, constantly bringing to mind the forbidden thought or feeling. "The brain is constantly processing forbidden content just outside conscious awareness.

---

[84] Wegner, Daniel M., and David J. Schneider, "Paradoxical Effects of Thought Suppression," Journal of Personality and Social Psychology, psycnet.apa.org/index.cfm?fa=buy.optionToBuy&id=1987-33493 -001, accessed July 7, 2014.

[85] Moss, Simon, "Ironic Rebound Effect," Psychlopedia, Oct 10, 2008, www.psych -it.com.au/Psychlopedia/article.asp?id=133, accessed June 20, 2014.

The result: You become primed to think, feel, or do whatever you are trying to avoid."[86]

Trying not to think of something makes you primed to think of it. To make matters worse, the more emotionally charged the thought, the harder it is to suppress[87] *and* the more persistent the thought the more likely you are to assume the thought is true. To stop this train wreck:

- Avoid working creatively in a way that encourages analytic thought and then requires you suppress (throw away) any thought about the work.
- Accept any persistent thought. It's just a thought, it can't hurt you.
- Question whether the content of the thought is valid. For example, it's been a rough day on set with a difficult scene and right before you hear "Action!" the thought, "I can't get this right," pops into your head. Do not try to suppress the negative thought. Instead, question whether the thought is true. You will probably realize that there is nothing inherently or inevitably true in the negative thought. Accept the thought, invalidate the content, and move on. Even if the content of the thought is inarguably valid, you'd do better accepting the thought or feeling than trying to suppress or deny it.

Study on positive self-talk

A recent study published in the *Journal of Personality and Social Psychology* found that subjects who performed positive self-talk in the *third person* could "influence their ability to regulate their thoughts, feelings, and behavior under social stress, even for vulnerable individuals."[88] The

---

[86] McGonigal, Kelly, The Willpower Instinct: how Self-Control Works, Why it Matters, and What You can do to Get More of It (New York: Avery, 2012).

[87] Jeremy, Dean, "Why Thought Suppression is Counter-Productive," PsychBlog, May 22, 2009, www.spring.org.uk/2009/05/why-thought-suppression-is-counter-productive.php, accessed July 7, 2014.

[88] Kross, Bremner, et al. "Self-Talk as a Regulatory Mechanism: How You Do it Matters," American Psychological Association, February 2014, www.ncbi.nlm.nih.gov/pubmed/24467424, accessed March 9, 2014.

study concludes that self-talk in the third person is more effective than self-talk in first person. That is, "I am a good actor," isn't nearly as effective as the same statement expressed in the third person: "(Your name) is a good actor."

Earbuds and waiting rooms

Music is a wonderful tool for actors in audition waiting rooms. Many actors prefer music without lyrics and download orchestral soundtracks befitting the score for the type of role and the project, and listen via earbuds in the waiting room before their audition. Audition waiting rooms are often anxiety inducing, even if actors claim they don't get nervous at auditions. Aside from your own possible twinge of performance anxiety, and hearing the casting director and other actors through the wall, many other actors waiting are quietly nervous, reading their lines and nervous, or chatting nervously. Feelings are contagious. It's a lot like talking to someone who is sniffling, coughing, their nose is running, their face is sunken and pale, they keep insisting they're fine—and you know you're going to catch it. The best defense against catching nerves is to tune everyone out with your earbuds with music that can set the mood for your character and story.

Enjoy the process except when you don't

It's important for the mental health and creativity of any artist to allow and accept what you are feeling, even and especially if it's considered wrong. The main difference between being a professional artist versus making art as a hobby is that, as a professional, you can't quit when your art gets painful and uncomfortable. When art is your profession you have to deliver to survive. Getting outside your comfort zone, pushing yourself beyond where you'd like to quit, is how you learn and grow. Not every moment is a cakewalk.

If making art is making you chronically miserable, that's another matter. Enjoying the process is important but is often oversimplified with *shoulds* in the form of aphorisms that imply any degree of unhappiness means you're not doing it right. Parents talk about how much they love their children and the meaning being a parent brings to their lives. That doesn't mean that every day of parenting is enjoyable. Enjoy the process and allow for times when you don't.

Belief and Performance

I F the idea of building a strong self-image does not appeal to you, I suggest looking into certain philosophies that can help steel you against the pressures inherent in this industry and a life full of strife in general. Taoism, Buddhism, and Stoicism are some prominent ancient philosophies that offer modes of being in the world that subdue the volume of the ego, self-image, and nattering inner critic. In fact, a comprehensive overview of peak performance would be remiss without addressing certain benefits associated with faith.[89] I do not want to presume or discount the existence of a deity in bringing up this topic. The neurobiology of religious experience is not about the existence of God, but rather about the effect faith has on us. I think it's worth scientific and personal exploration to determine whether a strong feeling of majesty may be a key to tapping into something powerful just outside your self-awareness center. Feelings of awe, faith, and inspiration, and experiences associated with a higher plane of reality may allow us direct access to resources buried within the mysterious back channels of our minds.

A shortage of these emotional experiences may leave us at risk of overidentifying with an analytic, conceptual, thinking identity, borne of and trapped in a remarkable yet limited region of the brain. Neuroscientist Dr. Andrew Newberg, a pioneer in the study of the neurobiology of spiritual and religious experience, recently shared with the

---

[89] Syed, Matthew, Bounce: Mozart, Federer, Picasso, Beckham, and the Science of Success (New York: Harper, 2010).

Telegraph insights on brain scans of the limbic system, an area of the brain that regulates emotion. This area showed an increase in activity when people were engaged in meditation and prayer. But there was also a decrease in the parietal lobe, the area of the brain that orients you in space and time. Newberg states, "When this happens, you lose your sense of self."[90]

"The most beautiful thing we can experience is the mysterious. It is the source of all true art and science. He to whom the emotion is a stranger, who can no longer pause to wonder and stand wrapped in awe, is as good as dead. His eyes are closed."

Albert Einstein[91]

Ritual

Unlike routines, which are purely functional and often carried out on autopilot, rituals are associated with something meaningful and emotionally galvanizing. Ritual connects you to something outside the mundane. In an article in *Scientific American*, authors Francesca Gino and Michael I. Norton write, "Recent research suggests that rituals may be more rational than they appear. Why? Because even simple rituals can be extremely effective...What's more, rituals appear to benefit even people who claim not to believe that rituals work."[92] Actors have historically been ridiculed for simple-minded rituals and superstitions.

[90] Smith, Julia Llewellyn, "What God Does to Your Brain," Telegraph Media Group, June 20, 2014, www.telegraph.co.uk/culture/books/10914137/What-God-does-to-your-brain.html, accessed June 24, 2014.

[91] Einstein, Albert, Ideas and Opinions, based on Mein Weltbild, edited by Carl Seelig (New York: Bonzana Books, 1954).

[92] Gino, Francesca, and Norton, Michael I., "Why Rituals Work," Scientific American, May 14, 2013, www.scientificamerican.com/article.cfm?id=why-rituals-work, accessed March 9, 2014.

This is sad, because actors have instinctively tapped into a largely un-acknowledged and potentially limitless brilliance, though not the same kind of brainpower deemed of worth by modern Western society.

There are Only Three Possible Mistakes

"With every mistake we must surely be learning."

George Harrison[93]

Mistakes are necessary. Embrace them, laugh at them, and be grateful for them. They are your number one beacons of progress.

1. It's only a mistake if you don't acknowledge your mistake

Confusing our words happens as a natural part of human conversation. In fact, slipups in auditions and performances can shake you out of autopilot and inject fresh impulse and spontaneity into the scene. This even works for comedy if you're rooted in a strong comedic character reacting spontaneously to what comes up in the moment. Periodically a so-called mistake will help you win a role. But these are happy accidents, not *real* mistakes. Real mistakes are not acknowledging a mistake. Don't bet that nobody noticed, or that everyone probably understands what you really meant, or that the lines don't matter. It makes

---

[93] Lennon, John, G. Harrison, and P. McCartney, "While My Guitar Gently Weeps," The White Album, November 22, 1968, Apple Records.

it look like you're reading lines without trying to convey meaning—something that never happens in real life. We are constantly checking ourselves and those with whom we are speaking to make sure we conveyed our meaning effectively. I am not advising you break character, abashedly stopping the scene, and asking to start over. Remain in character and acknowledge your mistake as your character would. It doesn't take more than a beat or two to say what you meant.

Of course, every once in a while it's simply necessary to stop the verbal diarrhea and start over. Breaking character by laughing at yourself relieves the asymmetry of fear that creeps into your face when you realize everything's going south fast and you can't figure out how to save it. Authentic laughter, not nervous laughter, is key here. One LI actress I know never worries about being perfect in auditions and regularly has everyone laughing along with her when she screws up. Her ease and joy is infectious. She's got a great attitude and works all the time. Laughing it off defuses any tension in your body and in the room. It also suggests to others that you are easygoing and fun to work with.

2. It's only a mistake if you don't learn from your mistakes

If you leave an audition feeling like you've truly messed up, set aside some quality time to spend with your mistake. When the pressure is off, identify the exact nature of the blunder. Was it nerves? Sloppy speech? A lack of commitment to character? Overlook no details. Extract what insights you can from it. Perform a visualization of a future situation where you have used the lessons from the mistake to achieve a desirable outcome. Once you've learned all you can from it and have corrected your course, you must discard the mistake. Think of a thoroughly culled mistake as a slice of orange that you've nursed all the juice from, and what's left is rind and grit. At this stage, it is no longer a mistake. It's the excrement of progress waiting to be discarded. Old, empty mistakes are mind waste. There are two common and valid reasons for recalling or reliving a past mistake. First, take a moment to determine if there are any useful insights trying to make themselves known to you. Sometimes we get so scared to face our mistakes we don't make the most of them. If there's any useful remnant, acknowledge it, and practice making the corresponding adjustment on-camera.

When past mistakes have outlived their usefulness yet keep surfacing, you may be experiencing the first stages of the phenomenon of choking. It reflects your working memory on overdrive, panicking, making it almost impossible to glean insights from your mistakes and move past them effectively. Start working with the methods outlined in this book to give your working memory a rest.

3. It's only a mistake if you don't make any

Mistakes are the most valuable learning currency you have. If you are making a bunch of them consider it a time of great opportunity. If you find yourself in a cycle where you can't seem to break out of doing terrible work, know how frequently this happens to actors on the cusp of a creative breakthrough. One of the things that frustrated me about acting classes was how little tolerance is given to those wading in creative muddy waters. I witnessed repeatedly how teachers would distance themselves from a dedicated actor doing really bad work for periods extending into months. I understand that a student who is continually producing weak work can threaten the teacher who may feel the student's bad work reflects their teaching. But this usually leads to a dedicated student feeling as though they either failed, or the particular course of study failed them—when it is quite possibly neither of these.

Your brain is working things out in ways that aren't making themselves obvious to you. Keep disciplined, keep experimenting, don't let yourself get too frustrated, and don't be afraid of producing stunted work for a while. It's a necessary stage when making creative progress.

* * *

"Sometimes a smooth process heralds the approach of atrophy or death."

Neil Young[94]

---

[94] Young, Neil, *Waging Heavy Peace: a Hippie Dream* (New York: Blue Rider Press, 2012).

DIALOGUE

To memorize or not to memorize

WHEN actors have memorized their lines, it's called being *off book*. When actors haven't memorized, it's called being *cold*. Among the handful of contentious debates concerning acting, a most notable one is whether or not an actor should be off book and memorized in auditions. Casting directors, directors, and teachers fall on different sides of this issue. Some insist it's detrimental to an actor's performance to try to be off book in auditions, while others go so far as to insist that the actor's *job* is to memorize.

The answer is whatever works. The yardstick for whatever works is whatever yields your strongest on-camera performance.

When working with actors preparing for auditions, or roles in upcoming projects, or filming auditions to submit to casting, I started to see a pattern. The first few cold reads were interesting and fairly strong even if the actor was tripping over some lines here and there (without denying the mistake—see last chapter).

Being cold means you aren't anticipating or planning anything. Everything you are doing is fresh and interesting, even if it's not clean. When actors came back a day or two later memorized to get a clean take, the work was often considerably worse than the work they were doing when they were cold.

What all too frequently happens when you work at memorizing your lines and try to retrieve these lines in an audition is that you may look like you are delivering lines devoid of all meaning. At worst, you may deliver your dialogue emphasizing the wrong word, with a strange inflection, or screwing up the tenses, and speaking in ways you would never in real life. This is so common Michael Cera satirizes it in his web series *Clark and Michael*.[95] The scene begins at 0:40 of episode 10. You can see it in the reference section at www.TheScienceOfOnCameraActing.com.

Although this can happen to actors at any level, for more experienced actors the effect often isn't as obvious, which can be a trap for working actors who are really good at memorizing. The lines may be delivered perfectly and the read might be really good, but it's just not great. It's missing something. What's missing are the subtle impulses that come to you when you're not *trying* to reach for dialogue, when you are in character and the dialogue is effortlessly coming to you, and all you're doing is reacting in the moment.

When editing the work of actors who have tried to commit their lines to memory in the short period of time before an audition, you can see what's happening frame by frame. You might see in one frame the eye suddenly widen and you can see all the white around the iris. In that one single frame, a split second before the actor hits on the line, the actor leaks fear. But it's so subtle it's often only exposed by a micro expression. Most people don't detect the detail. They just offer their overall impression that the performance is good but not great.

I was working with an actress who picks up her lines very quickly, but she has this tell that gives her away. For a fraction of a second her eyes—not her eyelids but her actual eyes—flick slightly upward when she's trying to retrieve a line. She's not aware of it while it's happening, and it may happen a few times throughout a scene. I can only catch the subtle action while editing, because it's only in one frame. Even in that one frame, it's very slight. I wasn't convinced of what it was until we

[95] Cera, Michael, "Clark and Michael – Episode 10" YouTube video, 0:40, posted by CBS, April 21, 2009, www.youtube.com/watch?v=TnS_YRCaJGI, accessed July 6, 2014.

watched it together and she confirmed that she was trying to retrieve a line.

Playback at normal speed gives the viewer the impression that the actor is good, but the performance isn't grabbing them. In these situations the casting director is just going to pass. Often the suboptimal performance is attributed to the actor not being prepared, when in fact the problem is the actor is overly prepared and creatively hogtied.

It takes time for memorized dialogue to root itself so you can retrieve it effortlessly. There are environmental and biological factors that go into determining how long this can take. So it's not entirely in your control. While you may have memorized your lines by the time you have your audition, they may not be available to you in a way that frees you up creatively as much as you may think.

But there's a way of learning dialogue other than rote memorization, reading it over and over until it's devoid of all meaning. Alternatively, you can passively pick up your lines through a process called **acquisition**. Linguist Stephen Krashen[96] observed that people learn language better through immersion than sitting in a classroom. If you want to learn French you're going to fare a lot better spending time in France interacting with French speakers than spending years learning vocabulary, syntax, and semantics in a class. Krashen's model of acquisition learning is a good model for actors and dialogue. Acquisition involves passively learning your lines through meaningful interaction. In other words, it's important that you learn your lines through naturally communicating them to the other character, by being immersed in the context of the dialogue—by getting on your feet and working on your scene.[97] The best route for learning dialogue is to acquire the dialogue naturally and emotionally. Emotion enhances our memories. This is

---

[96] Schütz, Ricardo. "Stephen Krashen's Theory of Second Language Acquisition (Assimilação Natural - O Construtivismo No Ensino De Línguas)," June 12, 2014, www.sk.com.br/sk-krash.html, accessed August 9, 2014.

[97] You don't need another actor for passive acquisition of your lines. It's just as effective to acquire dialogue on your feet, working out your scene to a mark on the wall. Your imagination will suffice to create the other character. Simply leave space for the other character's lines. Read through the whole scene so you have an understanding of what the other characters are saying to you.

the case for better or for worse. The boredom or pressure you may feel when you're working at memorizing your lines can actually affect how you retrieve them later on. The dialogue risks sounding contrived and you've saddled yourself with a new task of having to reanimate it. Multicamera comedies are ideal for acquisition because they're the closest thing to the rehearsal time you get working in theater. You're on your feet with your fellow cast members, having fun, working through the blocking, trying things out. You're more likely to acquire your lines because the scene is in context: rehearsing all week and then taping at the end of the week.

In the first section we discussed two kinds of trying: helpful vs. unhelpful trying. The constructive kind of trying is trying something new for experimentation and discovery. The counter-productive kind of trying involves struggling for results. A PLOS ONE study suggests it is more challenging for adults to acquire a new language than for children because once cognitive capabilities are fully developed, grown-ups often try too hard.[98] "'The most surprising thing about the study is that trying can actually harm learning outcome," Amy Finn, a postdoctoral researcher at MIT's McGovern Institute for Brain Research."[99]

The best way to acquire your lines without the negative effects of effort is to first learn a good line-reading technique. A line-reading technique is a technique for reading dialogue cold off the page. It isn't distracting to your audience, and you can focus on character and being in the moment instead of the lines. I recommend Margie Haber's line reading technique. I'm sure there are others out there, but I learned hers and it's been the single most useful skill I ever got from an acting class. She teaches weekend intensives in Hollywood, California, or you can get the formula from her book *How to Get the Part without Falling*

[98] Finn AS, Lee T, Kraus A, Hudson Kam CL (2014) When It Hurts (and Helps) to Try: The Role of Effort in Language Learning. PLOS ONE 9(7): e101806. doi:10.1371/journal.pone.0101806 www.plosone.org/article/info:doi/10.1371/journal.pone.0101806, accessed August 1st 2014.

[99] Dickerson, Kelly, "Why Adults Struggle to Pick up New Languages." LiveScience. www.livescience.com/46938-why-adults-struggle-with-new-languages.html, accessed August 1, 2014.

Apart![100], which outlines the technique in a few pages in the chapter "Reading in Phrases." It's simple to learn and only takes a couple weeks of daily practice to master. Once mastered, the line-reading technique becomes an implicit skill, meaning it requires no conscious effort. It's second nature. And your sides are there for you so you don't risk the microflash of panic the camera sees when you're reaching for a line in an audition and you have no backup.

Actors with a solid line-reading technique who are trained on-camera are able to pick up sides cold and nail the audition in under fifteen minutes. I see it with every actor who works this way. Their work is full of fresh impulses because they haven't tried to memorize. By working creatively on-camera, they pick up most of the dialogue meaningfully through acquisition, and only seamlessly go down for lines every once in a while, if at all. As you become more practiced with this process, your line-reading technique paired with the nonanalytic approach outlined in this book will allow you to be mostly or even entirely off book for auditions via an organic process that bypasses working memory.

This comes back to the directive prescribed by cognitive scientist Sian Beilock: "Employ learning techniques that minimize reliance on working memory to begin with."[101]

There is, of course, an exception that proves the rule. Although you usually want to avoid the deadness of meaning inherent in rote delivery, with comedy deadening the meaning means deadening your reaction to the humor. This can be worked to your advantage. As discussed earlier, in a comedy you mustn't behave as though you are aware that you are delivering funny dialogue. If you kill the comedy for yourself by repeating the dialogue while trying to memorize it, you may actually be affixing a more deadpan delivery.

---

[100] Haber, Margie, and Barbara Babchick, How to Get the Part, without Falling Apart! (Los Angeles: Lone Eagle Pub., 1999).

[101] Beilock, Sian, Choke (Carlton, Victoria: Melbourne University Press, 2011), 60.

Sleep

If possible, avoid working on your audition the day of your audition. Ideally, put a good night's sleep between your preparation and the audition. While you sleep, your brain takes the important information and separates it from the noise and irrelevant stimuli from the day before. If you work on the material the same day as your audition, you're reintroducing noise. This distracts and disconnects you from the moment, even in subtle ways that you may not be aware of. If you have a same-day audition, fitting in a fifteen-minute nap between the prep and the audition can really help. Of course, I encourage you to test this for yourself.

Work on your audition the night before using the approach outlined in this book until you're happy with it on-camera. Don't touch it the day of, and that's it. It's simple but it's not easy. It probably won't feel like you're working hard enough. And you might feel more confident and comforted working on your audition right up to the point where you're going over your lines in the waiting room. But just because it feels better doesn't necessarily mean your performance will be better for having done this.

Having worked with innumerable actors, watching and editing their on-camera work, Krashen's acquisition model and the cognitive science behind how we learn is pretty consistent with everything I've observed. Even if it feels counterintuitive you may still want to give this a try.

Music stand

Years ago, when filming auditions in a medium shot or close-up, I began using a music stand with a large piece of foamcore. I set the stand at a thirty-degree angle and laid the foamcore down where the sheets of music go. Foamcore is an inexpensive, lightweight piece of polystyrene foam sandwiched between sheets of glossy-white, thinly laminated paper. Foamcore below your face bounces available light, preventing the camera from picking up exaggerated and unflattering shadows of the face cast by unbalanced overhead lighting. A single piece can compensate for the horrible fluorescents in so many offices where auditions are held. Like a musician, the music stand also allows you to perform hands-free even if you don't have your lines memorized. Many actors I coach fold the top of their sides and place their lines over the foam core, as seen in the image below.

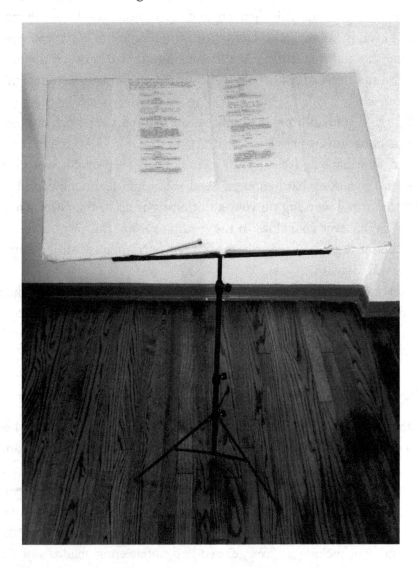

When you need to grab a line, your eyes won't disappear off-camera if you simply give a casual glance just below frame to the top of the foamcore where your lines are waiting. The stand also has the additional benefit of keeping your feet rooted on your mark so you don't drift off -camera right or left.

This tip works when you are self-taping auditions to be submitted to casting. I've also used it on set when going in for an actor's coverage. My students have said they wish they could bring a music stand and piece of foamcore to their auditions, but it is not socially or professionally accepted in that capacity.

Field research

Passively acquiring your dialogue through a solid line-reading technique is validated by a number of real-world audition and on-set observations and experiences.

Being more relaxed about your audition is the style in Los Angeles, where a working actor is often auditioning multiple times a day and isn't likely to have time to memorize pages and pages of material each day. A prominent manager in Los Angeles told me that being off book risks sending the subtle signal that you probably aren't going on many auditions, and aren't really in demand.

One actress I worked with went for the final round with the casting director and creator of a show. She was reading for the role of an irreverent character and there were pages and pages of sides with long speeches. About three-quarters of the way through the audition the actress got to the end of a page and was in the middle of a speech when she looked up, shrugged, and said that she had to stop there because she'd run out of printer paper and couldn't finish printing all the sides. After a beat, the creator and casting director laughed, and she got the part. So here was an instance where what helped this actress get the job was not only being cold, and not even having all her sides, but owning the character.

Before I knew of Krashen's acquisition model, I had an unusually long speech to deliver for a TV series. I think of myself as a professional so I put a lot of effort into it. I worked the lines over and over so I could be off book and loose on the day. I performed the scene in one take and the entire crew stood up and applauded when I was done. You may have heard the old expression, if the crew liked it you sucked. Of course if you pull off a scene in one take, the crew loves you because they get to go home and they regard you as a professional because you regurgitated a mouthful of words without a glitch. Of course too, the crew is also watching your performance with their naked eye, and what works for the naked eye often doesn't work on camera and vice versa.

When this particular episode aired, my work was okay, but it was nothing special. Even though by the time I performed the speech the lines were coming without effort, it still wasn't as good as the first time I rehearsed it on-camera, cold. And this is because the way I memorized, going over and over the lines, actually narrowed my creative impulses with that particular sequence of words.

I've worked with actors who would be considered pretty unprofessional. They'd show up to work and have no idea what scene we were shooting that day or what their lines were, and they'd trip all over themselves while we're shooting. But when the episode airs, their performance cuts together beautifully. I've asked friends who work in film and TV, both in front of the camera and behind, particularly editors, and this is often something they've observed too, especially with series regulars on single-camera episodics. These actors, the stars of the show, are tossed pages of new dialogue every week or two, and then rewrites. They usually aren't off book even by the time the camera is rolling.

I shared this with my students, but they were clearly skeptical. Two weeks later one of my students guest starred on an episode of *The Mentalist*. This actor came back to class and told us that Simon Baker, an Emmy and Golden Globe nominated actor for his work on *The Mentalist*, was almost totally cold on-set. If you've seen *The Mentalist*, Baker's performances cut together exquisitely, and his choices and creative impulses are beautiful.

Along these lines, James Dean believed one of the keys to good acting was to never know your lines too well. Dean was off book as little as possible and never did a scene the same way twice. Marlon Brando wouldn't memorize either. He had an assistant feed him his lines through an earpiece. This sort of raises the question, is it really professional to be off book, and is an actor's job really to memorize?

Reading to an eyeline

Actors enjoy acting with other actors. Many actors are extroverts and part of the joy of the job is collaborating with others. I'm not saying don't work with other actors. What I am saying is learn how to act to a mark on the wall as your eyeline and discover you no longer need a real person to react off of. No doubt this sounds completely counterintuitive. It's advice that is met with the most resistance at first. An eyeline is either another actor, a tennis ball, a piece of gaffer's tape, or any real or imagined mark just off-camera designated to deliver your lines to. It takes no time to get comfortable acting to a mark. The only block is your own resistance. Every actor I've ever worked with, no matter how resistant initially, has come to embrace acting to a mark.

"I am enough of an artist to draw freely upon my imagination."

Albert Einstein[102]

---

[102] Einstein, Albert, "Is Imagination More Important than Knowledge? Einstein." Times Higher Education. November 8, 2002, accessed August 6, 2014.

An actress I was coaching couldn't stand this idea. She was a screen acting veteran and the mark was unsettling. She resisted it in every class, but I insisted she get comfortable with the mark and showed her that it made no difference in her on-camera performance. She went on location for a movie shoot in which she played James Caan's wife. One day they were shooting a scene in a pool. She was lying in a bikini on a raft in the middle of the pool talking to Caan who was standing on the deck. After shooting Caan's coverage,[103] he was rushed off set to prep for the next scene, leaving the actress lying on a raft in the middle of a pool for her close-up. The director asked her to speak her lines into the air somewhere above the pool, just off-camera. Usually this would have been a problem. But like so many actor problems, it actually wasn't. She put an imaginary mark in the air and acted her coverage to it without incident. She came back to class embracing the mark.

Experiment acting to a mark: have your reader sit wherever they are comfortable so long as the mike can pick up their lines. Place the mark anywhere that allows your face to open up to the camera. In this photo the mark is a tennis ball but it could just as easily be a piece of tape stuck to the wall.

The tennis ball in this photo is the eyeline closest to the lens (an iPad camera). The tennis ball is the character you will be speaking to most. If there are more characters in the scene, place imagined eyelines according to their character height. For example, if a character is a child, make sure the eyeline is placed low, but not so low that your eyes fall too far below frame. This is called an eyeline "cheat."

I recommend placing all the characters in the scene on either camera right or left, to avoid having your eyes cross the camera, putting you at risk of spiking the lens.[104] The exception to this is when your character is speaking to a large group, in which case don't bother with any marks. For large groups, it often works to simply imagine people spread out

---

[103] Coverage happens after the master shot, when the camera goes in for medium shots and close-ups.

[104] Spiking the lens is when you look directly into the camera, breaking the fourth wall.

just below the bottom of the camera's frame. Scan the imagined crowd as you speak.

The mark can be anything. Practice with a tennis ball, a piece of tape, or better yet, an imaginary mark you can line up so it gives you the best eyeline in any situation you find yourself. Mastery of this means you'll be the compassionate co-star letting your fellow actors go home after their coverage. This is especially useful when you're guesting on a show. The star (series regular) who works long days every day, is often shot out first so they can go home. It's a courteous gesture letting them go home if you don't need them to stick around to read with you off -camera for your coverage. And they may be unintentionally returning the favor by leaving.

How often have you heard an actor leaving an audition talk about how the reader wasn't giving them anything? Perhaps you've thought or said this yourself. Worse than the bored, deadpan reader is the overly zealous reader. In auditions, I prefer just about anything to a reader off -camera who is acting their heart out and distracting from the audition. Overzealous readers are usually actors interning for the casting director for the valuable experience of observing the casting process, while trying to snag a small role in the film. This sort of reader will often try to give you the stars and the moon to work off of, but really the effect is overdoing it and can become quite distracting. If you must act to another reader in an audition scenario who is not giving you much to work with, or giving you an avalanche, their head can easily be substituted in your mind with a mark, and it won't matter what they are doing.

I recently heard the story of an actress who tried to sabotage another actress (let's call the victim of the subterfuge Mary) by rehearsing in their trailers one way and then mixing it up when they were on-set doing Mary's coverage. It was apparently effective. Mary was thrown and had a hard time recovering during her close-up. Mary wouldn't have been shaken had she graciously suggested this thespian saboteur go relax at crafty while they finish Mary's coverage. I was once on-set with an actress positioned on a mark behind me who decided she wanted to steal the scene and went to work with laser focus, trapping imaginary moving specks in the cracks of the floorboards we were sitting on while I delivered my lines to a character off-camera. I didn't realize what was happening until the cinematographer pulled his head out from behind the camera, pointed to her and said, "I know exactly what you're doing, you're trying to steal focus." I turned around and the actress reddened. At this point in my career I was still struggling, finding my way through the art and politics of acting, and was rattled. But the allegiance of the cinematographer emboldened my confidence and I offered to help the actress with her imaginary task. Instead, she opted to abandon it. You'll be immovable when you're self-reliant, handling political pettiness and insecurity with grace, because no one will be able to take your scene from you.

Sliver of space

An effective communication habit you may want to experiment with and adopt for the camera is not letting your lips close completely once you've finished speaking your lines. Maintain the slightest sliver of space while you're listening to the other character. This is body language that compels in close-up. It's almost like your relationship with the other actor is connected via a gossamer thread flowing from your lips to theirs. If you close your mouth you sever the connection. When top and bottom lips touch, closing off any space, it can appear as though you are broadcasting the nonverbal message, "I'm done speaking now, and have somewhat checked out until my next line." Watch how this reads on-camera.

Of course, when you're playing a character who *has* checked out, perhaps someone who is less interested in communicating than dictating, or a narcissist who is dismissive or indifferent to those around you, closing your mouth when you are done speaking can be a wonderful choice. A bevy of dismissive activities while your lips lightly touch, like checking your phone, then asking how someone is doing in monotone while looking away says, "I'm engaging in social niceties but I don't care about you." These characters are really entertaining jerks.

Never overlap lines when shooting coverage

Established actors—and anyone who's ever directed—know how important this rule is, but I've seen less experienced actors ruin shoots and burn their own best take in independent films by a sheer lack of technological understanding. Do not overlap lines when you are shooting coverage. Overlapping is when you're trying to play the scene naturally by cutting off the other actor just a moment before they've finished speaking. You can overlap lines on a master shot where every character is in the frame with you, but you must never overlap lines when going in for close-ups. Natural overlapping in close-up shots is accomplished in editing. If you want your best close-up used in the final product, your director needs a clean take with no audio overlap so that they can match shots in editing.

Let's say a director and editor are in postproduction cutting a scene. Your co-star is just about to finish their last line when you start speaking, cutting off the last half word out of your co-star's mouth. The shot now has to cut away to you, but your close-up doesn't match the way you said your line when you overlapped your co-star's best take. The director loves your co-star's best take. So the director now has to choose to either remain on your co-star's face while you speak off-camera instead of cutting to you, or rejecting your best take in favor of one that matches.

Another note buried in this tip is to hang out in an editing bay. You can PA, intern, shoot and direct your own short—whatever it takes to observe this process. You learn all your mistakes in editing, when you see how shots should fit together but can't because of something silly that never occurred to you while you were shooting.

VOICE

Dr. Ekman: "The voice is another emotion-signal system. Does it signal emotions clearly that the face does not? There's some evidence that the voice is the best signal system for feelings of sensual pleasure and contentment, much better than the face. People will give you a particular smile or a variation on a smile but it's not as clear which kind of enjoyment they're having. There is some work being done in England on voice being a primary distinctive signal for any kind of sensory pleasure and any feeling of relief. Also, we know the voice is a great signal system for amusement—the chuckle and laugh.

* * *

Many vocal training programs offered to actors today focus on opening up your pelvis, diaphragmatic breathing, relaxing, resonance, and staying hydrated. This is great, and you can find many classes dedicated to this kind of work. But it also seems that many successful screen actors today have very little vocal training. Screen actors don't have to project to the back row of a theatre. Acting in film and television is traditionally more of a visual medium than theater, where the emphasis is on the spoken word. And screen acting rarely ventures into the musical genre these days. Yet I'd like to focus on one specific area of vocal training that has great implications for every contemporary screen actor.

The perilous lack of speech training for screen actors reveals itself most obviously in the context of proper elocution and comedy. If you take the time to study comedies you'll notice the precision and clarity with which skilled comedic actors speak.

A while ago I started experimenting with tricks to sweeten audio when editing actors' online auditions. I noticed that if I used the actor's raw comedic performance that was fairly strong on its own and then bumped certain consonants, it gave the overall impression that the actor was an expert in the genre. I used the sweetened version to show actors how nuances of elocution and appreciation for the sounds words make suggest comedic proficiency. Consonants b, d, k, p, and t are *consonant plosives* that tend to lend themselves to humor because they involve a sudden kick, a release of air. This is called *phonosemantics*, the idea that sounds have inherent meaning.

The claim that consonant plosives lend themselves to humor does not mean that humor is boiled down to phonemes, only that some sounds support comedy more than others. A notable comedic master of language and sounds was George Carlin, who listed the kumquat as a food that sounded too funny to eat, and whose wildly celebrated monologue *Seven Dirty Words You Can Never Say on Television* (replete with plosives) was so celebrated and controversial it made it all the way to the United States Supreme Court.

Smoke and mirrors

I filmed an actor for an audition who performed excellently, but at the end of his strongest take he dropped the consonant on the last line, which sort of hollowed out the full impact of the closing beat. One interesting fact about memory is how important it is to end strong, because the impression that ingrains itself in memory is the beginning and end of an event. When I captured the footage to edit I tweaked the audio track, isolating and bumping the consonant, shaving off the edges of any background hiss so the consonant played smoothly. It took a mere two minutes of sound mixing and I did it in front of him so he could see the difference before and after and the importance of a strong ending. Although this actor had plenty of experience, having just starred in a summer blockbuster (and yes, still having to audition), he was silent as he processed the overall impact of this one little tweak. He shook his head, "It's all smoke and mirrors…"

Dustin Hoffman speaks openly about one of the most famous scenes in film history, the movie that put him on the map, *The Graduate*, with Anne Bancroft. During the shooting of this scene, Director Mike Nichols whispered to Hoffman to walk over and put his hand on Bancroft's breast. Bancroft didn't miss a beat and ignored Hoffman's hand while fussing with a stain in the pleat of her dress. Hoffman said he had to turn and walk away from camera and bang his head against the wall to keep from laughing and breaking character. In the film, the effect is of Hoffman's character, Benjamin Braddock, having a complete emotional breakdown. A magnificent scene, an incredible film, and my point is that even if you're a marvelous actor, it doesn't take away from the fact that film is a lot of smoke and mirrors. Talented actors just bring more smoke and bigger mirrors.

…As do gifted editors. I worked with an editor some years back who talked about a show she was working on with an actress who won an Emmy for her performance on the show. The entire staff in postproduction unabashedly takes credit for this actress's Emmy because the actress is notoriously difficult and not very capable. To salvage each shot, production ordered directors to keep the cameras rolling between takes. Every time the actress stood on her mark, waiting to hear "action," goofing around, talking to her friends in hair and makeup (strategically positioned off-camera) the cameras rolled, and the show's editors used countless of these very natural moments caught on film as reaction shots to insert into scenes in the actual show. The trick worked better than they expected.

Proper elocution

It's not just comedy that requires proper elocution. While watching several deftly written and performed dramas on TV, my husband and I (both with perfectly good hearing) are frequently unable to catch critical, plot-twisting lines from supporting cast members, and sometimes even the series leads. Actor mumbling is nothing new, but it's especially distracting when the shows are so good you truly care about every line being uttered. Fine actors swallow words all over the place, confusing otherwise superb performances.

One evening I was rewinding my DVR to catch a muffled word breathed through barely parted lips and clenched teeth. Frustrated I abandoned the television program and did a YouTube search and landed on the channel Elocution Solution featuring an exceedingly straightforward YouTube video on elocution. A list of words and phonetic sounds on a screen and a small box in the upper-right-hand corner framed the face of a New Yorker guiding me through proper jaw, tongue, and breath placement for words I had no idea I'd been mispronouncing. I contacted the woman featured in the video, certified speech pathologist Harriet Pehde. I signed up for a series of Skyped elocution lessons with her and downloaded her elocution video handbook, which I highly recommend.[105] I found it helpful and inexpensive, and speech pathologists Harriet and Ann are warm and pretty adorable.

The key to perfecting today's preferred style of acting, naturalism, is to avoid mumblecore[106] performances and to perfect the soft, articulate throwaway. Learning this involves reconditioning oral habits. Practice elocution exercises slowly and intentionally, and commit, for the sake of practice, to overenunciating. Once the habit has been internalized —delivered from working memory to procedural memory—you can vocalize with more subtlety and still be understood. It goes back to the old adage: you must know the rules before you can break them.

---

[105] I have no affiliation with any material, people or organizations I've recommended (other than my own) and do not benefit from endorsing them.

[106] I believe it was the Sundance Film Festival that coined the term mumblecore to describe a trend of acting in independent films where dialogue was mumbled.

Common mispronunciations in the standard American dialect

Many English speakers in North America think elocution involves fully pronouncing the t sound (aspirating) or hitting the t sharply. An example of this is pronouncing the t in *kittens*. This is, in fact, a mispronunciation that makes the word *kitten* sound pretentious or silly.

It is correct to pronounce the t in words like *articulate*, *abstract*, and *attract*. However, in words like *kitten*, *identity*, *reality*, *and personality*, the t is pronounced more like a d. How often have you heard someone try to sound intelligent and refined by mispronouncing the t in these words? You may crave the opportunity to work with great writing, but would you know how to articulate great writing? Not to seem like a slap on the back of the hand with a ruler, but a large part of an actor's job is to beautifully and effectively transmit the words in a script to the audience. Proper elocution is necessary to convincingly portray a wide range of roles, and is necessary for almost any period piece as elocution was a core curriculum in elementary school until this past century.

Proper elocution, when spoken subtly and expertly, sounds beautiful. It's pleasing to the ear. Your voice has the potential to sound attractive while sounding natural, modern, edgy, or relaxed. The adoption of a formally affable voice doesn't preclude the option of turning it off at will. Breadth requires mastery. Mastery requires practice. Practice elocution.

For a sample of a video tutorial from the elocution handbook see the reference section at www.TheScienceOfOnCameraActing.com

The musical notes of words

In unrehearsed conversations, the emotion and meaning you wish to express informs the impulse, pitch, and stress patterns of your speech. This enhances meaningful communication. Pehde describes it as words having musical notes.

* * *

Harriet Pehde: "There are two types of examples [of the musical no-tation of words] that come to mind. One is the intonation and stress patterns of a word, where you would use different pitches on different syllables to color the meaning of a word, and different levels of stress on a syllable. An unstressed syllable would be like an eighth note and a stressed syllable could be a half or a whole note depending on how much you want to stress it. For example the word 'important'—Depending on the context, each syllable could be stressed the same, or the 'im' could be the eighth note and the 'port' could be the half note and the 'ant' would be another one-eighth note. Another example is that each sound in a word has an assigned beat and if you leave out a sound or add an extra sound the timing is off and it falls flat. Just like when you're off key. Take the same word 'important'—if you produce the first t with too much air, the word is choppy and doesn't flow properly."

* * *

You've likely attempted to memorize lines by rote, standing in front of a mirror practicing your delivery, trying to infuse the lines with just the right, most compelling emphasis. In other words, you've used working memory to rehearse the pitch, stress, and pace you thought would best affect the delivery of your lines. However, this flips a natural process on its head. Instead of the meaning plucking the chords of your words, music is made in the hopes of bringing about meaning. This often limits actors as it leaves them relying on form, not content.

It can also lead to a director wanting, nay, *needing* to give you a line reading. A line reading is when the director reads the actor's lines show-ing them the tone, inflection, and delivery that they wish the actor to reproduce. There is a moratorium on line readings that actually under-scores a major barricade to actor-director communication, particularly when actors have rehearsed their lines by rote. The confused etiquette that directors cannot give actors line readings may disrupt the mutually desired outcome of both actor and director: a strongly communicated performance. Unfortunately, the practice endures, mainly because it is thought of as threatening or pejorative to actors.

A line reading from a director is seen as a major faux pas, an insult to actors and the mark of an amateur or unprofessional director. The general feeling is if a director does not like how the actor is performing so much so that they feel a need to give line readings, they shouldn't have cast that actor.

But the blackout on line reading paints the practice with too broad a brush. Line readings are often the most effective and unambiguous means of showing an actor when they are missing the musicality of a phrase, the proper inflection, which occurs routinely, usually as a result of the actor rote memorizing lines. You can mispronounce a phrase like you'd mispronounce a single word. In both cases the result is distracting and weird. Actors mispronounce phrases all the time. By repeatedly practicing variations on delivery, the actor divorces the sound of words and phrases from their underlying message. This is when a director needs to give you a line reading to get the train back on the track. But because line readings are frowned upon, the director talks in circles to describe what could so easily be demonstrated.

Pehde used the example, "Hi, how are you?" to point out the common musicality of phrases. There are a handful of various inflections that work for this phrase, like the classic inflection, the monotone, and the staircase. The classic inflection is the pitch on the word "are" in "how are you?" is delivered higher than the "how" and the "you." Try inverting the classic inflection and the phrase sounds very weird and distracting. Play with the pitches in the inflection diagram and hear how the different inflections sound.

To be clear, an actor can deliver a line countless wonderful ways if the musicality isn't so off-key that it reveals a disconnect with the message, reducing the words to nothing more than noise. When the musicality of phrasing is off-key it is not the same thing as making an interesting, creative choice in your delivery. This is sometimes what actors, deaf to their muddled inflection, insist they are doing. When a director

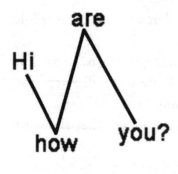

**Classic
inflection**

Hi, how are you?
_____

**Monotone
inflection**

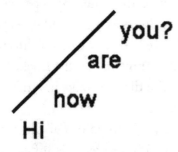

**Staircase
inflection**

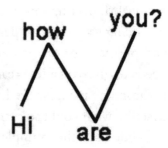

**Inflection that is
distracting
and weird**

shows an actor the difference in inflection, by delivering the line the way the actor is delivering it and then delivering the line with the proper musicality, the line reading works like a tuning fork for the actor. This does not have to be the director saying, "I want you to say it exactly like this," but, "I want you to be in harmony with the meaning of your words."

To expedite communication, perhaps we need a new, acceptable way of talking about the various uses of line readings. A director might offer an actor a "tuning adjustment" before giving them a line reading. Again, a talented actor who doesn't need to be told how to perform their role still may need to adjust their instrument every once in a while.

A true and meaningful performance has as much to do with emotion as it does with elocution. The greatest of jazz improvisers knew every angle of every note. They rehearsed for countless hours and played the scales over and over until they could twist those scales into any sound shape at any given moment. Writers do this with the written word. Actors do it through the spoken one. When a director says, "Great but can you try it like this?" you should find joy in playing with the concinnity of words and not feel pressured to play an unfamiliar instrument.

Accents

Accents are a great tool to distract working memory and liberate creative impulse. Occupying your analytic mind with the task of maintaining an accent lets inspiration breathe. Most actors report having an easier time acting when having to affect an accent. I have a theory that Australian and British actors fare so well in the United States in part because they are forced to put on an American accent for every audition. Provided you can pull off a convincing accent, this would give anyone a competitive edge.

Your native tongue shapes your face

Human beings hold their faces in different ways according to their native language. As an example, you've likely heard (in general terms) that French women have a sensual, feminine guile. France's Romance language requires the speaker's mouth to pull forward into a slightly pursed-lipped pout, somewhat as though the speaker is being kissed.

In contrast, English speakers in North America tend to pull back with the corners of the mouth when speaking.

Playing with different accents can shed light on how much of your face is based on more or less static factors like bone structure, or placement of muscles and ligaments, versus what is conditioned through a lifetime of speaking a certain way. If you don't like the way your mouth pulls back, or any other physical characteristic conditioned by a lifetime of repetition, you can go a long way in reshaping it through feedback from the camera and repetition to instill new, subtle oral habits.

Body

"The most fundamental question I think we can ever ask is why we and other animals ever evolved a brain. When I ask my students this question they'll say we have [a brain] to think or to perceive the world, and that's completely wrong. We have a brain for one reason and one reason only and that's to produce adaptable and complex movement. Because movement is the only way we have of affecting the world around us."

Dr. Daniel Wolpert, neuroscientist and professor at Cambridge University[107]

OUR brains did not evolve to keep us trapped inside our minds. For actors this is especially the case. The audience cannot read your thoughts, intentions, subtext, backstory, and motivations unless these are expressed verbally, by the ideas scribed by the writer or the behaviors and physiological cues of the actor. Your tools are your actions and reactions—whether conscious, unconscious, habitual, or impulsive—and your emotions, tears, laughter, saccades, fixations, nictations, etc. It does not end there. It does not end. Your tools are whatever reads on-camera, and hopefully you will continue to explore this indefinitely.

---

[107] Isser, David (Director), "Beyond the Wormhole with Morgan Freeman," Discovery Channel, 2013.

Character physicality

Research psychologist at Ohio State University Denis Schaffer[108] has shown that much of our daily movement that feels like conscious choice happens beneath the level of conscious awareness. Like voice and virtually everything else, the character's physical rhythm often emerges organically from these depths, as the actor experiments with an emotional throughline and the text. Physicality frequently emerges from impulse. Again, this is not a rule set in stone. You can also experiment on-camera with different movements and repetitive rhythms. What's right is what works.

Activities

Like accents, activities occupy working memory thereby freeing impulse. Make sure the activity has purpose, even if it is small. Pick an activity only if it is appropriate and natural for your character in that moment. For auditions pick an activity that doesn't involve any prop that you wouldn't have on you, for example, a pen, sides, cell phone, etc. An activity that works great in auditions is sorting papers, as you can use the sides in your hand; or trying to fix a piece of your attire, like buttoning, zipping or tying something.

React physically to your imagined environment

It took me a while before I realized the practical importance of this principle in auditions. Populate your environment with the imaginary objects that would be there in real life, then react to your environment. If you see it, the oddest thing happens: your audience sees it too. If a character in the scene calls to you from off-camera, acknowledge the direction from which they would be calling you, not from where your reader is sitting. If your character is shown a photo, use your eyes to place the pantomimed photo far enough in front of you and just below

---

[108] Ibid.

frame. This gives the illusion of the photo just below-frame in a way where the camera can still see your eyes. Cheat the photo, cheat your eyes.

Like with all rules, there are exceptions to this one. An actor I worked with placed the object they were referring to throughout the scene, behind them. In a sense, the imaginary object became an activity because the actor had to swing around 180 degrees every time he needed to reference the imaginary object. His back faced the camera as he cranked his neck over his left shoulder and strained to speak to the other actor off-screen. It was a great choice that helped define his awkward character.

Once you make an object real, respect the space taken up by the imaginary object. Once you've established where a table is located, do not walk through the table. This rule applies to every imaginary object you come into contact with in a scene. If a previously established imaginary object suddenly disappears from your hand as you turn the page of your script, the imaginary world you created evaporates in the minds of your audience. To avoid this, simply place the imaginary object down on an imaginary table before turning the page. I know it may seem like an easy thing to ignore, but test this for yourself and its importance should become apparent during playback.

Reboot

To shake up your impulses and shift out of autopilot when caught in your head and creatively skipping like a record, switch your feet. We often stand with one leg extended a bit further than the other, our weight shifted slightly to the other side. If you are standing with your right leg out a little further than your left, take a small jump and switch the position of your feet upon landing. Then go back into your scene liberated from this stilted state. You will find you are freer with your impulses and the dialogue.

Action in auditions

Action sequences can be difficult to play in auditions, where you're performing in the confines of an office space and don't want to look absurd as you pretend you're plummeting thousands of feet from the belly of a jetliner. Examples of common action scenes in auditions are car accidents where, say, the car goes careening off the side of a cliff after spinning across two lanes of traffic. Actors tend to carry on naturally during the scene until the car-crash cue, when they start whirling about in their chair. The actor will jerk back and forth and thrust about, playing the car wreck. The problem is that they're actually playing the role of the car. The car is flying all over the place. The natural human response is to stiffen up. It's a very small action. A reflex. It's a quick inhale, tensing your body as you brace yourself for the outcome. If your character is drunk the reaction will be slightly different. It's more of a sudden disorientation. Drunks aren't stiff, which is why drunk drivers are more likely to walk away from car accidents than sober drivers. Their bodies are loose upon impact. Yet as a driver or passenger, drunk or stone-cold sober, you are not auditioning to play the vehicle.

Colin Walk Forward

Through experimentation one of my students Colin Campbell invented *The Colin Walk Forward*. He became so familiar with where he stood in a frame that he could use a stationary camera on a tripod to create a medium shot that he would turn into his close-up at an important moment in the scene by taking two slow steps at a slight angle toward camera. He is now able to masterfully close out his audition on a compelling close-up shot.

Colin became so cognizant of his place in a frame and his eyelines that he frequently brings his lines condensed onto one page and a piece of tape to his auditions. He politely asks casting if he can tape his page just off-camera as an eyeline (he spent several classes training himself to take in the page as a whole without saccadding or squinting as he reads).

Colin reports that most casting directors have permitted this. He is then hands-free, with a teleprompter that doubles as an eyeline. He often auditions cold this way, delivering every line perfectly, spared any fleeting micro expression of anxiety that could leak onto his face from forgetting and having to search for the right word. His impulses are free as working memory is almost completely relieved of duty allowing him to slip seamlessly into the zone in his auditions. Colin says that he became a member of CAZT to perfect these techniques. CAZT is a casting office that films actors' auditions and uploads them to their website. Actors who are members are able to download the video of the audition they just had at these offices to see their work and get feedback (in a note written beneath the video) from casting. Colin says when he's been permitted to use his audition method it has always played back beautifully.

I share these techniques with some reservation because it's the type of thing an actor is likely to read about and try out in professional settings before becoming proficient. Be aware that this may agitate casting, which could cause the practice to become universally frowned upon. It's a joy being technically proficient enough to play with the tools of your trade as though they are extensions of your body. But technical mastery comes before agility and play.

Because few actors possess technical proficiency on-camera, actors must request permission, or such expertise can backfire. This happened to an actress who tried the Colin Walk Forward in an audition. A casting associate became alarmed and began frantically moving the camera trying to keep the actress in the medium shot as the actress stepped forward. So few actors are cognizant of the parameters of their frame that the associate assumed the actress was going to fall off-frame. In fact, this actress had a mastery of the frame, where she stood inside it, how much she could move without changing the composition, because it was second nature to her. Always ask casting if you'd like to make any minor technical adjustments or plan on moving within the frame.

An actor not understanding the edges of your frame is like a painter not knowing where to find the edges of their canvas. These are things actors must know blindfolded, and are some of the innumerable things that become second nature as you deepen your working relationship with the camera.

Your physique

So much has been said about diet and exercise, the only thing I wish to add is that one of the least dreary ways of staying in peak physical condition is to use exercise as a means of acquiring physical prowess. Add new skills to your repertoire like boxing, gymnastics, horseback riding, or circus training. You never know what obscure physical skill will give you the edge for a particular role, and it's fun staying in shape while discovering new things you can do with your body.

Makeup, hair, and wardrobe departments

"Actors work and slave and it is the color of your hair that can determine your fate in the end."

Helen Hayes[109]

I want to devote the rest of this chapter on body to your physical appearance on-camera as dictated by hair, makeup, and wardrobe (also called "vanities.") This is an area that I have never seen get much attention. Yet it is one I hear actors stress about, lament over, and shed tears over, after a day of work where they felt insecure on-set because someone responsible for their appearance made them look awful. I've

---

[109] Hayes, Helen, quote, n.d., Poem Hunter,
www.poemhunter.com/quotations/famous.asp?people=helen%20hayesl, accessed March 9, 2014.

worked with a top-of-field makeup artist who gave me Groucho Marx eyebrows and layered the makeup so thick I looked like a performance -ready drag queen when my character was a college freshman. These aren't even my words. A message board featured a lengthy thread about how I looked like a drag queen, and I couldn't disagree with any of the comments. An actress friend of mine was always finicky about her hair. Hair stylists on-set loved her full locks and would emphasize the boldness with big, fun styles. But it dwarfed her face on-camera, undermining her delicate beauty. In some instances her hair was a goofy distraction in scenes where her acting was superb and would have otherwise served as great clips for her reel. Even though she was fond of her natural tresses, she eventually had her hair chemically straightened to avoid the stress of having to assert herself with hair stylists with their own ideas while she tried to stay centered and in character. Another actor friend starring on a television show would sit in makeup for a half hour before returning to his trailer, where he'd wash off his entire face and then proceed to set. He said it was just easier that way.

Because actors are living, breathing, eating, moving canvases, a PA will call "final touches" on-set before the camera rolls, an expression used to cue vanities to do any final tweaking. This usually stirs up a flurry of activity around actors standing on their marks, and it's the best time for a makeup, hair, or wardrobe person to check a monitor and see what the camera sees. One day, in the makeup trailer, I cautiously tried to speak to a makeup artist who was caking it on my face. Another actress I was working with had encouraged me to speak with the makeup artist as she too thought I looked funny. The talk seemed unavoidably uncomfortable. Later, when I was standing on my mark and the PA called "final touches," the makeup artist looked the other way in a defiant gesture of "you're on your own." I later noticed older, more experienced actresses simply insisting upon what they wanted, forgoing any discussion of the matter. The amount of subversion that goes on between actors and vanities is nuts.

Another factor is that many makeup artists are still adjusting to the switch from 35mm film to digital HD. Informed and disciplined vanities recognize that newer cameras amplify. Makeup looks heavier, hair looks bigger, and wardrobe is louder or hangs differently on screen than it does in person. You'll notice many of these principles by experimenting with the camera. Patterns in clothing, jewelry, accessories, makeup, and hairstyles that work in person often overwhelm on screen.

Not all makeup, hair, and wardrobe people are created equal. And it seems truly talented artists are more impervious to feedback than their less-skilled counterparts. One of the best makeup artists I ever worked with, Zee Graham, turned to face me in the mirror when she was done and said, "If you've got a problem with anything, speak up." She chided, "It's your face being immortalized on celluloid, not mine." I was surprised and grateful she even asked. Few ever do. And the fact is, it is your face, your hair, your body. At the end of the day, the audience is more apt to think you are not physically appealing, not that makeup or hair screwed up. So be polite but assert yourself. No makeup, hair, or wardrobe person has lived with your face, hair, and body as long as you have. They did not make you up before the audition that got you cast. I've walked from a makeup trailer onto set and had a director freak out because I looked so much different than I did when I came into audition. Yet, oddly, I've never had a makeup or hair person confer with me about how I did my makeup and hair for the audition that got me the part.

* * *

Zee Graham: "Back in the good old days they had camera tests, a whole day devoted to creating the character's appearance and seeing how makeup looked on camera and what worked. It should be a collaboration of the director, actor, and hair, makeup, and wardrobe. It's rarely a collaboration of anyone these days. Concerns need to be voiced before the cameras roll so it doesn't become a complicated continuity issue down the line. Usually the only department an actor meets with before shooting is the wardrobe department when you go in for your fitting. Makeup and hair get sent notes from wardrobe and we base your look on what you'll be wearing. So you could always give your phone number to wardrobe to pass on to makeup and hair and ask them to call you. That way you can make a polite introduction and have a brief conversation about any of your concerns before arriving on the day."

* * *

Ideally, actors need to feel confident when they walk out on set. Even if you're playing a wretched-looking beast, you need to feel confident that you are the most fabulous putrid-looking beast. Part of makeup, hair, and wardrobe's job is to help get you into character, and not leave you stranded outside your center feeling self-conscious. But sometimes you need to set the stage for others to help you feel confident and grounded. Sometimes too, actors have terrible ideas, like one TV actress who was convinced an orange-tinged lipstick was her color. Or the actor playing the supernatural villain who 'borrowed' a thick charcoal eyeliner, and snuck into the bathroom to give his eyes some definition before shooting.

* * *

"It blows me away that everyone is so passive aggressive," laughs Zee. Zee's advice: "Don't come in with guns blazing telling your makeup artist how it's going to be, and don't let the makeup artists steamroll you either. Make a human connection. Hold out your hand to shake theirs so they don't have a spare hand to pick up a brush."

* * *

Exercise interpersonal skills. Juggle kindness and assertiveness to strike that balance so necessary for creative collaboration. You cannot do your own look, your own final touches, check the monitor, and keep track of continuity. You need a good working relationship with vanities. As Zee says, "It all boils down to confidence. If you're confident about what you want and you tell me, I will do it for you and I will probably do it better than you."

Part IV

Epilogue

DIY Filmmaking

IN early November 2008, my agent called with an appointment at Sony studios to meet with director Kevin MacDonald, who'd been forwarded my self-tape for the role of Sonia Baker in his upcoming film *State of Play*. At the time, the film's stars were Brad Pitt and Edward Norton. I was told I wouldn't have to audition again, the online audition my agent submitted was enough. Kevin blocked out Sonia's scenes and we verified availabilities for the Washington, DC shoot dates in December. It was the eve of the 2007 to 2008 writers' strike, and I was relieved something might come through before the looming dry spell.

But Pitt requested script changes. At midnight on November 5, the strike was struck; no more changes could be made. Pitt dropped out. Norton dropped out. The role of Sonia Baker went to another actress, but the role was largely cut out anyway. This would have been more frustrating if some variation of it hadn't happened countless times before, to myself, and every actor I know. Only now I was in a position where I had verifiable evidence my auditions were strong, so the realization that the traditional route is more chance than skill really hit home.

On the heels of the strike came the global recession. Employment pretty much came to a halt for anyone in Hollywood who worked in scripted. In the midst of widespread creative frustration, I bought a truckload of camera equipment (never do this—rent), set up an editing bay, produced and directed an improvised spec pilot, and fell in love with every aspect of filmmaking. Through casting, I better understood the audition process. By editing, I learned the ideal performance elements for editing a scene together. The experience also ingrained a profound respect for the actor's voice and the art of audio capture and sound mixing.

At this point it dawned on me that this business is like a Rubik's Cube. You have to keep cranking it until eventually the color squares line up. It takes a lot of time, creative thinking, and patience, and the DIY route allows you to peel off some of the stickers and put them where you want.

I recently had lunch with two young women in their third year at one of the most prestigious acting programs in North America. One of the women was describing her passion for every area of filmmaking in front of and behind the camera. But she had been given some advice from a university counselor citing some arbitrary or archaic policy that you have to choose between working in front of or behind the camera. Working behind the camera provides an invaluable perspective of the business and art of film acting. There is no better place to learn, and pay your rent, than on the job. In 2012, I worked for an executive who ran a major studio and I saw Hollywood's fabricated rules crumbling under the ever-sharpening scrutiny of common sense. The bottom line: if you are pursuing your goals with integrity you can do anything you want as long as you don't apologize for it. And never apologize for learning.

In 2012, my iPhone 4S with a FiLMiC Pro app was a better camera than the Panasonic HVX200 that was state-of-the-art and shot many independent films back in 2008. The iPhone plus the app combined were less than a sixth of the price. Editing software is soon coming to phones, and I recently heard the CEO of a postproduction firm talk about how his entire field will be obsolete in the next ten years as most editing will be done in real time in the cloud. In the few months since I started jotting down notes for this chapter, the technology has already gone through a new evolution. For this reason, I will forgo specifics about DIY filmmaking. Google searches within the past year will yield more relevant information on technology and trends. I also suggest you reach out to others interested or already working in film. Following the DIY route is becoming ubiquitous. Within a dime's throw are people in your area who want to tell stories with cameras.

"Film will only become an art when its materials are as inexpensive as pencil and paper."

Jean Cocteau[110]

I am not suggesting any actor forgo the traditional route. I am pointing out that at the time of publication, many actors, even actors with good agents, run into difficulties just getting seen by casting. The traditional route of struggling for the opportunity to petition others for work via auditions leaves actors with a lot of frustrating downtime that could easily be diverted into more productive and creatively fulfilling endeavors that complement the traditional path.

In dedicating myself to cracking the code behind a modern, practical acting technique, I fell in love with filmmaking. Yet in this area, I am still quite a novice. Learning all over again from this new perspective, I hope to have an update with more techniques to help actors in future editions of this book or through articles on my website www.TheScienceOfOnCameraActing.com. In the meantime, I encourage you to work with the camera, experiment with this approach,

---

[110] Cocteau, Jean, quote, n.d., www.jeancocteau.com, accessed July 7, 2014.

test it against others, build on it. Surround yourself with trusted advisors who can watch your on-camera work with you and give you constructive feedback. Keep honing your craft in a no-nonsense, evidence -based way of experimentation and observation. In no time you will meet the criteria of breadth and consistency that define what it means to be a talented screen actor. I wish you success and look forward to seeing your work.

BIBLIOGRAPHY

Aalto University, "How Emotions are Mapped in the Body," ScienceDaily. www.sciencedaily.com/releases/2013/12/131231094353.htm, becs.aalto.fi/~lnummen /participate.htm, accessed July 6, 2014.

Adler, Stella, in interview, "Stella Adler on the Stanislavski Method," YouTube.com video, posted by Orco Development, December 18, 2012, www.youtube.com /watch?v=LlvnBrE9wCI, accessed July 6, 2014.

Alter, Adam, "The Powerlessness of Positive Thinking," the New Yorker, www.newyorker.com/online/blogs/currency/2014/02/the-powerlessness-of-positive -thinking.html, accessed July 7, 2014.

Andjelkovic, Ivana, "Brain Tag," UC Santa Barbara, n.d.,

mat.ucsb.edu/~ivana/200a/background.htm, accessed March 9, 2014.

Association for Psychological Science, "Greater Working Memory Capacity Benefits Analytic, but Not Creative, Problem-Solving," ScienceDaily, www.sciencedaily.com/releases/2012/08/120807132209.htm, accessed July 6, 2014.

Barry Kaufman, Scott, "The Real Neuroscience of Creativity: Beautiful Minds, Scientific American Blog Network," Scientific American Global RSS. blogs.scientificamerican.com/beautiful-minds/2013/08/19/the-real-neuroscience-of -creativity/, accessed July 6, 2014.

Baum, Kenneth, *The Mental Edge: Maximize your Sports Potential with the Mind -Body Connection* (New York: Berkley Publishing Group, 1999).

Beilock, Sian, *Choke* (Carlton, Victoria: Melbourne University Press, 2011).

Berger, John. Ways of Seeing: Based on the BBC Television Series with John Berger. (London: British Broadcasting Corporation, 1990).

Bernstein, Adam (Director), "My Life in Four Cameras" *Scrubs*, YouTube, 22:40, posted by ABCTVONDEMAND, Jun 23, 2012 www.youtube.com/watch?v=4aNFrI7jpZI, accessed July 6, 2014.

Bois, Jon, "Tony Gwynn, Baseball Scientist, has Died," SB Nation, June 16, 2014, www.sbnation.com/mlb/2014/6/16/5814622/tony-gwynn-died-hall-of-fame-padres, accessed June 16, 2014.

Brickman, P., D. Coates, and R. Janoff-Bulman, "Lottery Winners and Accident Victims: is Happiness Relative?" Journal of Personality and Social Psychology, August 1978, www.ncbi.nlm.nih.gov/pubmed/690806, accessed March 9, 2014.

Bridges, Jeff, and Philip Seymour Hoffman, "Jeff Bridges." *Interview Magazine*, July 1, 2004, www.maryellenmark.com/text/magazines/interview/907I-000 -007.html, accessed August 6, 2014.

Caine, Michael (Director), Acting in Film, Tmw Media Group, 2007, DVD.

Capra, Frank, quote, IMDB.com, n.d., www.imdb.com/name/nm0001008/bio?ref_=nm_dyk_qt_sm#quotes, accessed March 9, 2014.

Cera, Michael, "Clark and Michael – Episode 10" YouTube video, 0:40, posted by CBS, April 21, 2009, www.youtube.com/watch?v=TnS_YRCaJGI, accessed July 6, 2014.

Cocteau, Jean, quote, www.jeancocteau.com, accessed July 7, 2014.

Conway, Martin A., "Memory and the Self," Journal of Memory and Language, October 2005, www.sciencedirect.com/science/article/pii/S0749596X05000987, accessed July 7, 2014.

Coyle, Daniel, *The Little Book of Talent: 52 Tips for Improving Skills* (New York: Bantam Books, 2012).

Day-Lewis, Daniel, quote, "First Look: Steven Spielberg, Daniel Day-Lewis and Sally Field," Oprah's Next Chapter," www.oprah.com/own-oprahs-next -chapter/How-Daniel-Day-Lewis-Found-Abraham-Lincolns-Voice-Video, accessed July 6, 2014.

Dickerson, Kelly, "Why Adults Struggle to Pick up New Languages." LiveScience. www.livescience.com/46938-why-adults-struggle-with-new-languages.html, accessed August 1, 2014.

Doolittle, Peter, "How your 'Working Memory' Makes Sense of the World," www.ted.com/talks/peter_doolittle_how_your_working_memory_makes_sense_- of_the_world.html, accessed July 6, 2014.

Duhigg, Charles, *The Power of Habit*, April 17, 2012, charlesduhigg.com/flowchart -for-changing-habits/, accessed March 9, 2014.

Duhigg, Charles, *The Power of Habit: Why We Do what We Do in Life and Business* (New York: Random House, 2012).

Durant, Will, *The Story of Philosophy: the Lives and Opinions of the Greater Philosophers* (New York: Simon & Schuster, 1926).

Einstein, Albert, *Ideas and Opinions, based on Mein Weltbild, edited by Carl Seelig* (New York: Bonzana Books, 1954).

Einstein, Albert, "Is Imagination More Important than Knowledge? Einstein." Times Higher Education. November 8, 2002, accessed August 6, 2014.

Ekman, Paul, and Wallace V. Friesen, *Unmasking the Face: A Guide to Recognizing Emotions from Facial Clues.* (Cambridge, MA: Malor Books, 2003).

Ekman, Paul, *Darwin and Facial Expression: A Century of Research in Review.* (Cambridge, MA: Malor Books, 2006).

Ekman, Paul, *Emotional Awareness: Overcoming the Obstacles to Psychological Balance and Compassion: A Conversation between the Dalai Lama and Paul Ekman.* (New York: Times Books/Henry Holt &, 2009).

Ekman, Paul, *Emotions Revealed: Recognizing Faces and Feelings to Improve Communication and Emotional Life. Revised/Expanded ed.* (New York: Henry Holt, 2007).

Ekman, Paul, *Telling Lies: Clues to Deceit in the Marketplace, Politics, and Marriage. Revised/Expanded ed.* (New York, NY: W.W. Norton, 2009).

Emerson, Ralph Waldo, *Society and Solitude: Twelve Chapters* (Boston: Fields, Osgood & Co., 1870).

Engelmann, Jan B., C. Monica Capra, Charles Noussair, and Gregory S. Berns, Expert Financial Advice Neurobiologically "Offloads" Financial Decision-Making under Risk, PLOS ONE, March 24, 2009, www.plosone.org/article/ info%3Adoi%2F10.1371%2Fjournal.pone.0004957, accessed March 7, 2014.

Ericsson, Krampe, and Tesch-Romer, "The Role of Deliberate Practice in the Acquisition of Expert Performance," Psychological Review, 1993, www.nytimes.com/images/blogs/freakonomics/pdf/ DeliberatePractice%28PsychologicalReview%29.pdf, accessed March 7, 2014.

Ferrell, Will, and Paul Fischer, "Will Ferrell - Cranky Critic® StarTalk - Movie Star Interviews." Will Ferrell - Cranky Critic® StarTalk - Movie Star Interviews, accessed August 6, 2014.

Finn AS, Lee T, Kraus A, Hudson Kam CL (2014) When It Hurts (and Helps) to Try: The Role of Effort in Language Learning. PLOS ONE 9(7): e101806. doi:10.1371/journal.pone.0101806 www.plosone.org/article/info:doi/10.1371/journal.pone.0101806, accessed August 1st 2014.

Gino, Francesca, and Norton, Michael I., "Why Rituals Work," Scientific American, May 14, 2013, www.scientificamerican.com/article.cfm?id=why-rituals -work, accessed March 9, 2014.

Greenfeld, Liah, "Modern Emotions: Aspiration and Ambition," Psychology Today. www.psychologytoday.com/blog/the-modern-mind/201304/modern -emotions-aspiration-and-ambition, accessed July 7, 2014.

Haber, Margie, and Barbara Babchick, *How to Get the Part, without Falling Apart!* (Los Angeles: Lone Eagle Pub., 1999).

Hare, Robert as quoted by Mizzie Jones, "Mask of Sanity," February 19, 2009, masksofsanity.blogspot.com/2009/02/stare-of-psychopath-whats-beneath-it.html, accessed March 7, 2014.

Hayes, Helen, quote, n.d., Poem Hunter, www.poemhunter.com/quotations/ famous.asp?people=helen%20hayesl, accessed March 9, 2014.

Healy, Melissa, "Memories Can't Always be Trusted, Neuroscience Experiment Shows," Los Angeles Times, July 25, 2013, www.latimes.com/news/science/la-sci -implanted-memories-20130726,0,3603431.story, accessed March 9, 2014.

Hornby, Richard, *The End of Acting: a Radical View* (New York: Applause Theatre Books, 1992).

Hughes, Virginia, "How Scientists are Learning to Shape our Memory," Popular Science, www.popsci.com/article/science/how-scientists-are-learning-shape-our -memory?dom=tw&src=SOC, accessed July 6, 2014.

Isser, David (Director), "Beyond the Wormhole with Morgan Freeman," Discovery Channel, 2013.

Jeremy, Dean, "Why Thought Suppression is Counter-Productive," PsychBlog, May 22, 2009, www.spring.org.uk/2009/05/why-thought-suppression-is-counter -productive.php, accessed July 7, 2014.

Jones, Mizzie, Mask of Sanity, February 19, 2009, masksofsanity.blogspot.com/2009/02/stare-of-psychopath-whats-beneath-it.html, accessed March 7, 2014.

King, Stephen, Good Reads, Inc 2014. www.goodreads.com/quotes/23315-a-tragedy -is-a-tragedy-and-at-the-bottom-all, accessed August 1, 2014.

Kostarelos, Kostas, "I Have a Dream, that One Day Scientists and Philosophers will Join Hands," theguardian.com, www.theguardian.com/science/small -world/2013/dec/19/scientists-philosophers-sciences-humanities-nanotechnology, accessed July 6, 2014.

Kross, Bremner, et al., "Self-Talk as a Regulatory Mechanism: How You Do it Matters," American Psychological Association, February 2014, www.ncbi.nlm.nih.gov/pubmed/24467424, accessed March 9, 2014.

Kuleshov, Lev, "Kuleshov Effect" YouTube video, 0:45, posted by esteticaCC, March 10, 2009, www.youtube.com/watch?v=_gGl3LJ7vHc, accessed July 6, 2014.

Lennon, John, G. Harrison, and P. McCartney, "While My Guitar Gently Weeps," The White Album, November 22, 1968, Apple Records.

Lennon, John, "The Artwork of John Lennon." Exhibit - Fort Lauderdale, FL. Accessed August 6, 2014.

Lerner, Harriet, "Fear vs. Anxiety, the Dance of Connection," Psychology Today, www.psychologytoday.com/blog/the-dance-connection/200910/fear-vs-anxiety, accessed July 7, 2014.

Liroff, Marci. "Committing the Ultimate Hollywood Sin." Hollywood Journal. December 9, 2013, accessed August 8, 2014.

Luethi, Mathias, Beat Meier, and Carmen Sandi, "Stress Effects on Working Memory, Explicit Memory, and Implicit Memory For Neutral and Emotional Stimuli in Healthy Men," Frontiers in Behavioral Neuroscience, 2.

Macnab, Geoffrey, "The Madness of Daniel Day-Lewis—a Unique Method that has Led to a Deserved Third Oscar," the Independent, www.independent.co.uk/arts-entertainment/films/features/the-madness-of-daniel -daylewis-a-unique-method-that-has-led-to-a-deserved-third-oscar -8510704.html, accessed July 6, 2014.

Mamet, David, *True and False: Heresy and Common Sense for the Actor.* (New York: Vintage Books, 1999).

Mankiewicz, Joseph L. (Director), All About Eve, 20th Century Fox, 1950, DVD commentary.

Marano, Hara Estroff, "Our Brain's Negative Bias," Psychology Today, www.psychologytoday.com/articles/200306/our-brains-negative-bias, accessed July 7, 2014.

McGonigal, Kelly, *The Willpower Instinct: how Self-Control Works, Why it Matters, and What You can do to Get More of It* (New York: Avery, 2012).

Mitchell, Elvis, KCRW The Treatment with Elvis Mitchell, June 3, 2013.

Morris, Eric, and Joan Hotchkis, *No Acting, Please.* (Los Angeles, CA: Ermor Enterprises, 2002).

Morris, Eric, *Being & Doing: A Workbook for Actors.* (Los Angeles, CA: Ermor Enterprises, 1981).

Moss, Simon, "Ironic Rebound Effect," Psychlopedia, Oct 10, 2008, www.psych -it.com.au/Psychlopedia/article.asp?id=133, accessed June 20, 2014.

Nakano, Tamami, Makoto Kato, Yusuke Morito, Seishi Itoi, and Shigeru Kitazawa, "Blink-Related Momentary Activation of the Default Mode Network while Viewing Videos," Proceedings of the National Academy of Sciences of the United States, August 26, 2012, www.pnas.org/content/early/2012/12/19/ 1214804110.abstract?sid=9bd3b79a-ffdd-4057-8459-8be8d4a53bd1, accessed March 9, 2014.

Newman, Paul, "Newman Gets Animated for New Film." Reuters - TVNZ. June 7, 2006, accessed August 6, 2014.

Nordqvist, Joseph, "Intelligence Agents More Likely to Make Irrational Decisions Compared to College Students," Medical News Today, July 10, 2013, www.medicalnewstoday.com/articles/263107.php, accessed March 7, 2014.

Pagel, Mark, "Creativity, Like Evolution, Is Merely a Series of Thefts." Wired UK. March, 2014. www.wired.co.uk/magazine/archive/2014/03/ideas-bank/mark-pagel, accessed August 6, 2014.

Parker, Corey, "Paula Strasberg, Coaching Marilyn Monroe," memphisactor.blogspot.com/2012/12/paula-strasberg-coaching-marilyn -monroe.html, accessed July 6, 2014.

Picasso, Pablo, "The Artist Pablo Picasso" www.theartistpablopicasso.com/pablo -picasso-painting-Les-Demoiselles-dAvignon.htm, accessed July 6, 2014.

Racca, Anaïs, Kun Guo, Kerstin Meints, and Daniel Mills, "Reading Faces: Differential Lateral Gaze Bias in Processing Canine and Human Facial Expressions in Dogs and 4-Year-Old Children," PLOS ONE, April 27, 2012, www.plosone.org/article/ info%3Adoi%2F10.1371%2Fjournal.pone.0036076, accessed May 21, 2014.

Randerson, James, "You Really Can Smell Fear, Say Scientists," the Guardian, www.theguardian.com/science/2008/dec/04/smell-fear-research-pheromone, accessed July 7, 2014.

Robbins, Tim, "Tim Robbins Director - Interviews." Industry Central, www.industrycentral.net/director_interviews/TR01.HTM, accessed August 6, 2014.

Schütz, Ricardo. "Stephen Krashen's Theory of Second Language Acquisition (Assimilação Natural - O Construtivismo No Ensino De Línguas)," June 12, 2014, www.sk.com.br/sk-krash.html, accessed August 9, 2014.

Seneca, Lucius Annaeus, and Sir Roger L'Estrange, *Senecas Morals by Way of Abstract. To Which Is Added, A Discourse under the Title of An After-Thought.* (London: Printed for T. Osborne, 1762).

Seuss, Dr., *Happy Birthday to You!* (New York: Random House, 1959).

Sevincer, A.T., G. Wagner, J. Kalvelage, and G. Oettingen, "Positive Thinking about the Future in Newspaper Reports and Presidential Addresses Predicts Economic Downturn," Journal of the Association for Psychological Science, November 26, 2013, pss.sagepub.com/content/early/2014/02/04/0956797613518350.abstract, accessed March 9, 2014.

Shaw, George Bernard, Good Reads Inc., 2014 www.goodreads.com/quotes/185935 -imitation-is-not-just-the-sincerest-form-of-flattery– , accessed August 1st 2014.

Showfax.com, a service offered by BreakdownsExpress.com, the official website where the bulk of casting notices are posted, allows actors in North America to download their sides for auditions.

Smith, Julia Llewellyn, "What God Does to Your Brain," Telegraph Media Group, June 20, 2014, www.telegraph.co.uk/culture/books/10914137/What-God-does-to -your-brain.html, accessed June 24, 2014.

Spolin, Viola, *Improvisation for the Theater: a Handbook of Teaching and Directing Techniques* (Evanston, Ill.: Northwestern University Press, 1963).

Streep, Meryl, and Graham Fuller, "Streep's Ahead." *Interview Magazine*, December 1, 1998. www.simplystreep.com/content/magazines /199812interview.html, accessed August 6, 2014.

Streep, Meryl and Wendy Wasserstein, "Meryl Streep," Interview Magazine, www.interviewmagazine.com/film/meryl-streep#_, accessed July 6, 2014.

Syed, Matthew, *Bounce: Mozart, Federer, Picasso, Beckham, and the Science of Success* (New York: Harper, 2010).

Tarantino, Quentin (Director), Kill Bill. 2004. (New York, N.Y.: Miramax Home Entertainment, 2004).

Vertov, Dziga, and Annette Michelson. Kino-eye: The Writings of Dziga Vertov. (Berkeley, CA: University of California Press, 1984).

Vinter, Phil, "People with Shifty Eyes AREN'T Dishonest…they're just thinking hard," Mail Online, www.dailymail.co.uk/news/article-2171330/People-shifty-eyes -ARENT-dishonest–theyre-just-thinking-hard.html, accessed July 7, 2014.

Wegner, Daniel M., and David J. Schneider, "Paradoxical Effects of Thought Suppression," Journal of Personality and Social Psychology, psycnet.apa.org/index.cfm?fa=buy.optionToBuy&id=1987-33493-001, accessed July 7, 2014.

Whipp, Glenn, "Matthew McConaughey's Advice for a Career McConaissance," www.latimes.com/entertainment/envelope/moviesnow/la-et-mn-matthew -mcconaughey-20131114,0,5190927.story#ixzz2rBzkrWhC, accessed July 6, 2014.

Wikipedia contributors, Ironic Process Theory, Wikipedia, the Free Encyclopedia, en.wikipedia.org/wiki/Ironic_process_theory, accessed July 6, 2014.

Wujec, Tom, "3 Ways the Brain Creates Meaning," www.ted.com/talks/ tom_wujec_on_3_ways_the_brain_creates_meaning#t-345306, accessed May 30, 2014.

Young, Neil, *Waging Heavy Peace: a Hippie Dream* (New York: Blue Rider Press, 2012).

CPSIA information can be obtained
at www.ICGtesting.com
Printed in the USA
LVHW010833100822
725609LV00008B/382